WHEN
POLITICS
BECOMES
HERESY

THE IDOL OF POWER AND
THE GOSPEL OF CHRIST

"Most Americans assume that the political right and left are total opposites. In contrast, Tim Perry calls them out as all too similar, both claiming ultimate allegiance from their devotees and willing to sacrifice their opponents. Like Faust selling his soul for power, contemporary evangelicals, dissatisfied with their marginalization in a secular world, jockey for status with either 'white' or 'woke' politics. With insight and passion, Perry calls evangelicals to repent of their political idolatries and be true to Christ. This book is a must-read for all evangelical pastors and scholars."

—MARK MATTES, theology and philosophy department chair,
Lutheran Bible Institute, Grand View University,
Des Moines, Iowa

"History repeats itself. Tim Perry diagnoses the echoes of ancient heresies in the predominant forms of cultural and political engagement in contemporary American evangelicalism. The great virtue in his analysis is that he studiously avoids the pharisaical sanctimoniousness that too often characterizes critiques of evangelicals. Rather, Perry knows that this physician must also be healed himself, and he speaks to his beloved fellow believers from a place of humility and solidarity. And he offers clear prescriptions for each error. Therefore, though the diseases identified are severe, we are not left without hope."

—JAMES R. WOOD, assistant professor of religion and theology,
Redeemer University, Ancaster, Ontario; teaching elder in the
Presbyterian Church in America; co-host of *The Civitas Podcast*,
produced by the Theopolis Institute

WHEN
POLITICS
BECOMES
HERESY

THE IDOL OF POWER AND
THE GOSPEL OF CHRIST

TIM PERRY

LEXHAM PRESS

Lexham Press, 1313 Commercial St., Bellingham, WA 98225
LexhamPress.com

Print ISBN 9781683598428
Digital ISBN 9781683598435
Library of Congress Control Number 2024949179

Lexham Editorial: Todd Hains, Ethan McCarthy, Katrina Smith, Mandi Newell
Cover Design: Gabriel Eason

24 25 26 27 28 29 30 / US / 12 11 10 9 8 7 6 5 4 3 2 1

This book is dedicated to TH and KA,
who, in very different ways,
brought this book to print.

CONTENTS

"Heresies perish not with their authors,
but like the river Arethusa, though they lose
their currents in one place, they rise up again in another."

Thomas Browne, *Religio Medici*, 1643

A PRAYER FOR
TRUTH AND PEACE
IN THE CHURCH

IN THE NAME of the Father and of the Son and of the Holy Spirit. Amen.

> And now, O sons, listen to me:
>> blessed are those who keep my ways.
> Hear instruction and be wise,
>> and do not neglect it.
> Blessed is the one who listens to me,
>> watching daily at my gates,
>> waiting beside my doors.
> For whoever finds me finds life
>> and obtains favor from the LORD,
> but he who fails to find me injures himself;
>> all who hate me love death. *Proverbs 8:32–36*

GRACIOUS FATHER, we humbly pray for your holy Christian church. Fill it with all truth in all peace. Where it is corrupt, purify it. Where it is in error, direct it. Where anything is amiss, reform it. Where it is right, strengthen and confirm it. Where it is in want, provide for it. Where it is divided and rent asunder, heal its breaches; for the sake of him who died and rose again, and ever lives to make intercession for us, Jesus Christ, your Son, our Lord. Amen.

PROLOGUE

"**S**o what's this book about?" In the past, that question has not been challenging; I have been able to state the thesis of my books in a sentence. This one, on the other hand, has not let itself to such a straightforward answer. So instead of a thesis statement, a prologue.

This book is a lament. The way the political polarization of our wider culture has been mirrored in our evangelical churches is ugly. Pick any hot button culture war issue, and you will find evangelical missionaries who think it is their job to bless it and convert the unconvinced to their cause. And if we fail to convince, then we publicly condemn.

It is a plea. Bring the infighting, well, back in. Whatever debates or discussions we evangelicals have, they need to be brought back inside and not aired on social or mainstream media. Like the Corinthians, whose childish conduct was so embarrassingly public to Paul, we are making a mockery of the gospel when we parade our divisions in front of the world.

It is a call. Let's relearn our primary language—that which is provided by Holy Scripture. If we're going to bring our debates back inside the tent where they belong, we need to learn to talk to each other in ways that, frankly, the world doesn't understand. Early Christians did this by deploying, among other techniques, the language of the apocalyptic. We need to relearn the language not only of biblical apocalyptic, but of the Bible.

It is a panarion. My longsuffering editor has objected to this word because of its obscurity, but I thought I could at least sneak it in here. The *Panarion* (meaning "breadbasket") is a catalogue of heresies and how to treat them written by Epiphanius of Salamis in the late fourth century. This book aspires to be a modern panarion, an attempt to show how the old heresies persist in our churches. Here a clarification is in order. I am not saying that certain segments of American evangelicalism are literally recapitulating the ancient heresies. I do not believe there are evangelical emissaries lurking in the halls of Congress with bags of money looking to purchase influence or status any more than I am asserting that some evangelicals are saying plainly that the Creator is not the God of Jesus (gnosticism) or that the Son was the preeminent creature (Arianism), and so on. I am saying that heresy, like history, repeats itself. Its inner logic remains a constant temptation and, if we're not careful, reasserts itself in ways that are, for those who know their history and heresy, distressingly familiar.

The heretical patterns that are repeated today may not have much to do with particulars, but they are nevertheless present:

an unholy desire to remain influential, an overidentification with contemporary culture, a temptation to turn the gospel into a message of moral improvement or social justice, turning God's kingdom into ours, demonizing those who disagree. These are the core issues that, in the end, make the classical heresies, heresies. The particulars false doctrines, which must inevitably fluctuate across time and space, flow from them. And their source? The refusal, even rejection, knowing or not, of the gospel.

Because we have lost our language, the God-given tongue with which to describe ourselves to ourselves, we have also lost Jesus. This book explores the ways the Jesus of the Scriptures and ecumenical creeds has been misplaced. The overlaps between the major early heresies and contemporary, politics-obsessed evangelicalism make this loss evident.

It is, finally, my last love letter to evangelicalism. The Spirit, as far as I can tell, has departed us. We are no longer the movement that inspired the global missions explosions, the Wesleys, or even Billy Graham. We are by every conceivable metric a mirror of American culture: affluent, banal, blind to sin, and deaf to the biblical calls to judgment and offers of grace. When I began this book, I hoped that "walking the sawdust trail" of repentance was still an option. In God's grace, it may still be. But as the book nears publication, I am less hopeful. The calls to repentance and faith remain in the text no longer to call the movement as a whole to its senses, but to encourage the few who have yet to bow the knee to Baal to remain faithful.

Chapter 1

ANOTHER ONE?

Relearning the Language of Heresy

As for the idols of the nations,
they are but silver and gold,
the work of human hands.
They have mouths, but they speak not;
eyes have they, but they see not;
They have ears, and yet they hear not,
neither is there any breath in their mouths.
Those who make them are like them,
and so are all who put their trust in them.

Psalm 135:15–18

"Of making many books there is no end" (Eccl 12:12)—so says the Teacher. Tell the truth: was this the first biblical reference that came to mind when you picked up this book? Yet *another* book on the state of evangelicalism? There really is no end. Nevertheless, here we are. Evangelicals—at their best and at their worst—are both biblicists and navel gazers, with the unhappy result that when it comes to navel gazing, we evangelicals read this verse as a prescription: "Our making of books about ourselves must never end." Evangelicals seem more eager than most Christians to write and read, sell and buy, more self-examinations, self-justifications, or self-flagellations than any other ecclesial community. As hard as it might be to believe both inside and outside the movement, thanks to near ubiquitous caricature of the unreflective evangelical in American popular culture, no external critic of evangelicalism can compete with us when it comes to criticizing our own. We are our own best and worst critics.

I strongly suspect that this disposition toward self-criticism is written into our ecclesial DNA. Modern Anglo-American evangelicals have been trying to discern just what's wrong with us since the movement began; it is *why* the movement exists. The movement once known as neoevangelicalism (now with the prefix dropped) began with the publication of Carl F. H. Henry's *The*

Uneasy Conscience of Modern Fundamentalism.[1] In it, the theologian, journalist, and cultural critic called his fellow fundamentalists to leave separatism behind. Instead of retrenching in holy huddles, he argued, authentically evangelical Protestants ought to engage with wider American culture for the sake of the gospel. From that book flowed *Christianity Today*, the National Association of Evangelicals, and any number of other publishing houses, colleges, and periodicals that have come to define us through the intervening decades. And all along, those books, magazines, educational institutions, and church and parachurch organizations have been plagued by the predictable question of whether, in pursuing such engagement, we have gone too far or not far enough. Only one self-examination, as far as I've found, has ever moved past the obvious question-begging to ask whether Henry's vision was even possible: Mark Noll's *The Scandal of the Evangelical Mind.*[2]

I read Noll's book shortly after its publication in the mid-1990s. Graduate studies in the United Kingdom afforded me a context from which I could enter Noll's work less defensively than perhaps I otherwise would have been. At the time I fancied myself as a part of the new cadre of evangelical theologians. With the best educations that the best universities could offer, we were about to take our place among a new generation of cultured despisers without sacrificing the faith that led us there to begin with. You can well understand, with such a prideful vision, how hard it was for me to read that, as Noll put it, the scandal with the evangelical mind was that there wasn't one!

Noll's readers of course know that his thesis was more nuanced than that. He argued that evangelicalism lacks an intellectual culture that encourages and rewards achievement in the life of the mind outside the fairly narrow confines of biblical studies and theology—and even these are sometimes regarded suspiciously. Thus, we can't claim many public intellectuals, Noll and a couple of others excepted. Wheaton and Biola aside, we don't build universities like the Catholics. And whatever husks they are now, we simply don't have the intellectual history and cultural cache of liberal Protestant denominations and institutions. Seventy-five years ago, Henry called us out of our ghettos. Thirty years later Noll asked, "Are we even up to it?" That question has yet to be answered.

Instead, we stick with what we know: self-criticism. Were this book an academic one, now would come the ponderous paragraphs with near-endless footnotes confirming that I have read all that ought to be read, listened to every podcast, and watched every video recording on the subject. Thank God, this is not an academic book! Evangelical that I am, I will take as my biblical cover for this lack of academic respectability the second half of the Teacher's instruction with which I began: "Much study is a weariness to the flesh" (Eccl 12:12). Granting the possibility (even probability) of idiosyncrasy, then, it seems to me that while the self-examination has continued unabated since Noll's seminal work, his question remains. Furthermore, the sheer number and kinds of evangelical self-examination now on the market constitute prima facie evidence of the question's perennial viability.

Just as Albert Schweizer hung a question mark over the quest for the historical Jesus with his own historical Jesus,[3] so Noll has levelled a question that undermines the publications that continue to be churned out. Which invites you, dear reader, to pose the question directly to me. If Noll is right (he is), and he is vindicated regularly by the very existence of this disposition (he is), why write another such book? Do we really need another one? The remainder of this chapter attempts an answer.

Niebuhr and the Signs of the Times

Let me start in an odd place: my most peculiar reading experience of 2021. That year marked the seventieth anniversary of the publication of H. Richard Niebuhr's *Christ and Culture*,[4] the classic mid–twentieth century attempt to discern the relationship between the church's Lord and her context. Noting the anniversary and having the extra time that Covid had given me, I pulled the book off my shelf and read it again. I was stunned. Sometimes a book is a classic because it freezes a moment in time and gives a unique glimpse into a particular cultural moment now past; sometimes this status describes a book's capacity to continue to speak today. *Christ and Culture* is a classic in both senses of the word. I'll come back to that in a moment. First a brief summary.

Christ and Culture offers a chronological taxonomy of the ways Christians have sought to engage their cultural surroundings: "Christ against culture," "Christ of culture," "Christ above culture," "Christ and culture in paradox," and "Christ

transforming culture." Niebuhr begins with "Christ against culture," with its radical call to separate the community of faith
from the world and to the world to convert to Christ. While
one might be tempted to think that Niebuhr has in mind the
staunchly separatist fundamentalists of his own day (the group
Henry called his readers to forsake in 1947), he doesn't. Instead,
his major example is the early Johannine communities, with their
insistence on strong community and world boundaries defined
by holiness and love. His choice of community is itself insight-
ful: Niebuhr thus signals that it is entirely possible to be "against
culture" without being hostile to it. But that's for another book.
We might call the culture in which the Johannine communities
found themselves "pre-Christendom." Its opposition is genuine, but it is not borne of rejection of the gospel. Rather, it is
defined by ignorance. It is a world in which the inside-outside
boundary is easily drawn. Early on, ethnically mixed Christian
communities may have had trouble figuring out whether they
were more Jewish or gentile (see the Epistle to the Galatians), but
there was no doubt that they were different. Neither Jew (and
therefore legally protected) nor Greek (and therefore swimming
easily with the current of the general cultural milieu), they stood
out. And John, both in his Gospel and his letters, helped the
communities under his influence understand why: a community founded on the pursuit of radical holiness and social bonds
defined entirely by self-giving love will inevitably stand out.

Because of its own best lights, "Christ against culture" didn't
survive. It failed because it succeeded. The little community

huddled in the locked room for fear of persecution in John 20 encountered the risen Lord, received the Holy Spirit, continued the mission of the Son, and converted even Caesar (something John himself—if indeed the evangelist, the letter-writer, and the revelator are the same author—did not foresee). Whether Constantine's conversion was authentic or not (or whether, as is more likely, it was complicated, just like such conversions are for most of us), when he bowed the knee to Christ he abdicated his authority as a son of the gods. When Christ took up his lordly and rightful position at the heart of culture, there was no more culture to oppose.[5]

This is not to say that Niebuhr was enamored by "Christendom"—he was far too Augustinian for that. Thus, in Niebuhr's taxonomy, there follow two overlapping and ultimately inadequate models. In the first, "Christ of culture," Christ was absorbed by the culture. Foreshadowed in the gnostics and coming to full expression in Peter Abelard, the gospel's radical call to conversion becomes instead the means by which the status quo is justified. In the ancient world, any number of gnostic sects invented a Jesus who was just another heavenly visitor. A demigod with secret knowledge, this Jesus easily joined the ranks of many such avatars of the ancient mystery religions. A millennium later in at least some influential corners of Christendom, Jesus came to represent the very best of Europe, even as he was emptied of his own specific, apocalyptic peculiarity. In the second, "Christ above culture," Christ remained at the heart of culture but retained his evangelical appeal. Instead of an apocalyptic preacher heralding the inbreaking of the kingdom, however, Christ became a cultural telos, consistently calling Europe forward to its best and highest ideals. What Niebuhr called "Christ above culture," we might call Christendom. If you are hard-pressed to discern the difference between "Christ of" and "Christ above," you're not alone. And that is the problem. We can articulate it in two ways. Either "Christ above culture" is inherently unstable and eventually collapses into "Christ of culture," or they are so porous as to become indistinguishable. Either way, "above" invariably devolves into "of." Christ is entirely captured by culture.

The two models left are both identified with the magisterial wing of the Reformation. Niebuhr presents Martin Luther as the spokesman for "Christ and culture in paradox." I confess that this notion is the hardest for me to unpack, but perhaps a story might work. While in grad school, I studied with a Lutheran minister who had, in years past, served as a Navy aviator in Vietnam. When pressed by his more pacifist colleagues about how he could sleep at night after dropping his ordinance indiscriminately on North Vietnamese fighters, Viet Cong guerillas, and civilians, he replied coolly, "There is no conflict between my duty to Christ and my duty to my country." The answer made no sense to my friends, whether they were Erastian Anglicans (for whom the church has a nationally established public role as the conscience of the nation) or radical liberal or anabaptist Protestants (for whom American culture in particular stood under God's judgment, not least for its warmongering). For him, however, having absorbed Luther's doctrine of the two kingdoms deep into his bones, it was a perfectly reasonable answer. God had appointed the church to govern men's souls and the state to govern their bodies; they simply cannot come into conflict. He dropped his bombs in the morning, dropped to his knees to pray for his enemies at night, and dropped thereafter into a peaceful sleep. Niebuhr countered that this ultimately fell into a dualism in which the gospel could never criticize public life, a criticism largely justified by the ineffective—indeed complicit!—witness of German Protestantism during the Nazi years.

This left Calvin and the Reformed tradition. The Genevan giant uniquely held forth the option that Christ did transform culture and could and would continue to do so. The solution would not be a withdrawal from public life, nor would it be an ineffective posturing that left it unaltered. Christendom would be reformed and always reforming by the light of the gospel. As is often the case with such taxonomies, Niebuhr left his own position till last, and not simply for reasons of chronology. The book's very structure suggests the inevitability and superiority of Niebuhr's own position. At the time of its publication, that inevitability was further underscored by the dominance of American Protestant Christianity across the country's cultural institutions.

And that is the first reason for *Christ and Culture*'s classic status. It ably represents a time in North American Christianity when the future really did look bright. In the reconstruction after two world wars, years in which the American empire was about to come into its own and remain convinced of its own benevolence, it seemed perfectly obvious that Christ was on the cusp of transforming American culture and, through it, the world. It was an era in which the president of the National Council of Churches could phone the White House confident of a response; when the moderator of the United Church of Canada could ask for a meeting with the prime minister, and the PM would clear his schedule. It was the high point of North American Christendom. Today, it's hard to imagine that there was ever such a time. Nevertheless, this was the era in which Henry, along with Billy Graham and Harold Ockenga, called fundamentalism out of its separatism to join in a culturally transformative vision not all that dissimilar to Niebuhr's. Yesterday, all our troubles seemed so far away. Today, there is no more implausible picture than what seemed perfectly obvious to all of them. Only seventy years ago the cultural landscape was very different, and an encounter with Niebuhr is a bracing reminder of just what has changed and how quickly.

Second, classic status is granted because *Christ and Culture* continues to speak today. There can be no doubt, however, that its message has changed. If "Christ against culture" arose in "pre-Christendom," then today Christians find themselves in a globally ascendant "post-Christendom." If "Christ against culture" ended because it succeeded, "Christ transforming culture" is ending because it has failed. Thus, a solid interaction with Niebuhr's optimism frees us to ask whether anyone remains interested in contending that Christ remains at the heart of the secular West. As John Milbank, David Bentley Hart, Rod Dreher, and, for longer and more trenchantly, Pope Benedict XVI have been saying now for fifty years, the post-Christian West allows for no "of" or "above," no "paradox," and certainly no "transformation." Instead, it sees Christ as an oppressor whose shackles it is finally ready to throw off. The once bright, now flickering light of faith among the old stones of American Christendom[6] allows us still to see, if we have eyes, that post-Christendom stands on a rejection of the gospel. It has all the paganism and none of the innocence of the Areopagan philosophers of Acts 17. And this means a glib announcement of the return of "Christ against culture" won't do. An opposition borne of ignorance was converted over three centuries; what will happen in a culture founded on Nietzsche's deicide?[7]

White, Woke, or Worldly?

While the future is known only to God, one thing can be said for certain: in the three-fourths of a century since its publication, Niebuhr's preferred model of transformation has been reversed. The culture has transformed the church (or at least the American evangelical movement). It is certainly true that our culture has absorbed Christ, even if it cannot remember or recognize having done so.[8] The post-Christendom that has rejected the gospel wants very much to retain vaguely Christian notions of justice and equality and to retain an evangelistic and apocalyptic zeal that rivals that of the first century but to strip it of the Christian particularities from which those calls first emerged and in which those calls took concrete shape (and, frankly, made sense).[9] Any number of writers have spoken of the overtly religious dimensions of contemporary culture. Sermonizing and calls for repentance and confession abound (though there are precious few announcements of grace). The desire for a society of justice and peace, which earlier generations would have called the kingdom of God, makes it evident that whatever post-Christendom is, its rejection of the gospel is not straightforward. Thus, the first part of my answer to the "Why another book?" question is, "Because times have changed radically, for the worse, and very few seem willing to see just how bad things are going to get." The problem with much contemporary evangelical self-critique is that it doesn't go far or deep enough.

This brings me back to the contemporary practice of evangelical navel-gazing. As bracing as Henry's first challenge was in 1947, and as revelatory as Noll's was five decades later, it seems to me their critiques came from inside the movement and were offered for the sake of its health—not unlike a doctor who keeps telling her patient he needs to lose thirty pounds and stop smoking for his own sake. Henry wanted evangelicals to engage with the world not simply for the sake of the unevangelized but also for the sake of the movement's internal coherence. An evangelicalism that was separate and insular was not centered on the gospel, which is, by definition, outward looking. It was an internal contradiction. Noll stands in the same tradition, calling evangelicalism to its better self, to a tradition that gave rise to, for example, Jonathan Edwards and the founding of Princeton University.

For Noll, intellectual engagement ought to be a twofold aspect of evangelical identity—to lack it is to fail to love the Lord with our minds; to neglect it is to neglect one crucial aspect of the Great Commission. Making disciples, after all, must include a readiness to give an apology for our hope (1 Pet 3:15).

More contemporary critiques strike me as being critically if not very subtly different. They no longer come from inside for the sake of those inside. Rather, the new critics easily adopt the language of the critical theorists of the left or of the aggrieved right, not least because of the religious echoes deeply embedded therein, and adapt it to scoring spiritual or theological points against their brothers and sisters. In the minds of the exvangelicals and deconstructionists on the one hand and the retrenchers and paleofundamentalists on the other, evangelicalism today is either too white or too woke. The facility—even enthusiasm— with which so many on all sides have adopted the language of identity politics, however, has thus far been largely left unquestioned. If we dared to ask why, perhaps we might find that the real problem is neither whiteness nor wokeness but plain, old-fashioned worldliness. As my grandmother might have put it, evangelicalism has no problem that a good trip to the altar wouldn't fix.

"Worldliness." "A trip to the altar." Both are examples of "evangelicalese," a language we have inherited and which embarrasses some of us. But I use them deliberately. As a community discerning its relationship with the larger culture in which it finds itself, evangelicalism has typically had a fairly clear set of boundaries established by practices (church twice on Sunday, prayer meeting Wednesday night, and youth group on Fridays); taboos (we don't smoke, drink, or dance, to say nothing of playing cards); and speech (replacement swears and stock words and phrases such as those above). Today, for good or ill, those boundaries are largely gone. If today's evangelicals recall Sabbath observance, we do so to congratulate ourselves for being freed from our parents' scrupulosity; we mock their temperance over a beer; their turns of phrase have become material for Christian comedians (does it get more evangelical than the term "Christian comedian"?). But whatever legalistic wrongs we're leaving behind, we are losing our language. And insofar as we are, we are becoming a mystery to ourselves.

Inside and Outside the Walls

Perhaps an appeal to holy Scripture will help unpack what I'm after. In 2 Kings 18 and Isaiah 35, we read of the fraught negotiations between King Hezekiah and his advisors on the one hand and the emissaries of the marauding Assyrians on the other. Language is a major issue: Will negotiations among the elite and announcements to the people take place in Aramaic or Hebrew? In the language "outside the walls," or "inside"? One way to think about the dynamic that I've been trying to sketch thus far has to do with a similar kind of evangelical bilingualism. Since 1947, we've known that in order to engage the culture we need to be adept at its talk, its shibboleths, and its triggers. For Henry, throwing up the walls was both impossible and useless. At the same time, in order to remain fully and truly ourselves, we need to practice our own language, preserve our own observances, even "sing the LORD's song in a foreign land" (Ps 137:4). There's no point in becoming conversant in the language of public life if in fact we evangelicals have nothing distinctive to say, nothing that's been nourished by our own language, faith, and practice. I'm not sure that very many of the newer critics understand the bilingualism that Henry and Noll could take for granted. Henry and Noll could talk to us about us in a language that was our own, even as they called us to become fluent in a different language so that we could offer ourselves in mission to the world. The new critics, right and left, having held insider language up to scorn or lost it altogether, and no longer speak to us about us in our words. They have only the language of the world. Their evangelicalism is a veneer for something more primal. They are, in short, worldly.

A final word on the language of the world in which late modern evangelicalism finds itself entangled. It is, in short, the language of politics. All the time. In the collapse of the domain once called the religious, that part of human life in which the great questions of ultimate value, reality, and ends were entertained, the political has increasingly filled the void. Politics is everything and everything is politics, to the point that, as Jordan Peterson has aptly observed, politics has become the new language of the transcendent, so that the news media we consume, the popular culture—movies, television, books, podcasts—we enjoy, even what we eat or drink must make a political statement. Fox or CNN? Chick-Fil-A or Burger King? Ben Shapiro or Rachel Maddow? As a result, it is of paramount importance to have the correct political view on every possible subject. To have the wrong view is not simply to be mistaken, it is to be evil, contaminated, sinful.[10] And where the old language balanced sin, judgment, and even hell with the language of grace, forgiveness, and repentance, there seems today no way to remove the scarlet letter once it has been affixed by the new Puritans.

That's why I wrote this book. In all the current Sturm und Drang of the intra-evangelical culture war, precious few are asking why calls to forsake either "woke" or "white" seem to outnumber those that advocate leaving "worldliness" behind, and by a disturbingly wide margin. Nobody, it seems, is comfortable asking why we're more comfortable writing and reading books that take the language of politics as foundational and the language of faith as mere rhetorical flourish. I'm not making an argument that this is in fact the case, not because it can't be made, but because it's so obvious as to make arguing it unnecessary. Rather, I'm taking the primacy of politics in contemporary evangelical self-critique as a given and trying to name the peculiar kind of worldliness this devolution entails and to suggest consequences that flow from it.

The Language of Heresy

The name I will use is *heresy*, and more specifically, *Simony*. I will elaborate on Simony in chapter 2. For now, let's focus on heresy. The *Catechism of the Catholic Church* helpfully defines heresy as "the obstinate post-baptismal denial of some truth which must be believed with divine and catholic faith, or it is likewise an obstinate doubt concerning the same."[11] Heresy is, first of all, post-baptismal. Leave aside the distractions about the mode and significance of baptism. For my purposes, it is enough to say that this means only a professing Christian can be a heretic. Second, it's obstinate. Stubborn, in other words. This highlights the Greek root of the term, *haresis*, which means, simply, a choice. To embrace heresy is to choose stubbornly to depart from what has been received. Heresy is as much the attitude in which it is held as its actual content. It is the obstinate assertion of *self-will* over against the mind of the church universal, *while* insisting that one nevertheless remains a Christian. In this regard, it is striking that 2 Peter's description of heretics focuses more on the perversity of their wills than the content of their errors (2 Pet 2:12–13). And third, it is a "denial of some truth which must be believed." To embrace a heresy is to deny some core aspect of the gospel. After chapter 2, I look at subsequent heresies and ask just what our affectation with politics might cost, now and in the near future.

Heresy is not a word that ought to be used lightly, and I do not do so here. In my Bible college days, *heretic* was a joking appellation directed against someone whose views on a particular subject were outside the mainstream. I am not joking now. I write from the conviction that many self-appointed evangelical critics have embraced heresy—a false teaching which, if followed to the end, will lead to the damnation of souls. They have done so obstinately and deliberately. And the consequences are dire.

When I was in seminary, my pastoral theology professor liked to say, "Refusal to pray leads to the inability to pray," and "The consequence of sin is more sin." After defining Simony as the peculiar heretical temptation for too many contemporary evangelical self-appointed prophets, the remainder of this book will lay out the consequences of embracing it and will do so with my old professor in view. I will try to convince you that the consequence of embracing heresy is more heresy. Like the demon who, upon finding the human host from which he was once expelled clean, ordered, and empty, invites seven spirits more evil than itself to reenter with it (Matt 12:45), so no heresy is content to come alone. If our temptation in this cultural moment is to embrace Simony, we will not merely embrace Simony. If we invite him in, the spirit of Simon the Magician will happily enter, but he will not come on his own. He will bring with him the ghosts of the old gnostics (chapter 3), Arius (chapter 4), Pelagius (chapter 5), and Donatus (chapter 6), with the result that we will have become 2 Peter's heretics: wills bent on satisfying disordered desires and rationality long lost.

At this point, I expect some readers are hoping I will name names or take a side. And I'm going to disappoint you, both here as this chapter ends and throughout the rest of the book. I want as many people as possible to read this book and if I name names, I will immediately halve my potential audience (at least). So there's a practical and frankly self-interested dynamic at work here. I am not going to restrict my audience by "black-hatting" up to one out of every two potential readers. But second, and much more importantly, one of the hallmarks of contemporary evangelical critics is a near-insufferable sanctimony. You know it well, I'm sure. It prays with the Pharisee of Jesus's parable in Luke 18:9–14, "I thank thee Lord that I am not like that sinner," whether that sinner is a MAGA hat-wearing Trumper or a *Handmaid's Tale* harridan. Like the Pharisee of the parable, those critics go home as unjustified as they were before they prayed. I really don't want to add myself to that number. So in all that follows, when I talk about heresy and about the temptation among evangelical critics to embrace it, I hope I have only one critic really in mind—me.

For that reason, each chapter includes a call to repentance, not in the simple sense of saying that we're sorry (though that is part of it) but in the truer and more complicated call to walk in a different direction. A rejection of Simony demands a renewed attention to prudence; rejecting gnosticism, to realism; Arianism, to incarnation; Pelagianism, to evangelism; and Donatism, to patience. And the only person I am qualified to call to repentance—to use inside language, to invite down the sawdust trail to the mercy seat—is me. But I hope that in the end, insofar as the call is genuine, mine won't be the only knees under the altar rail.

Chapter 2

SIMONY

Holy Spirit; Worldly Purpose

———————

Rapacious ones, who take the things of God,
that ought to be the brides of Righteousness,
and make them fornicate for gold and silver!
The time has come to let the trumpet sound
for you!

Dante, *Inferno*

In the previous chapter, I laid out the presuppositions on which this book is based. (1) Large swaths of North American evangelicals have lost the ability to speak and think in their internal language, either through disuse or deliberate neglect. (2) To compensate for that loss, they have imported the language (and deep convictions) of the world. Whatever internal elements remain, they increasingly borrow rhetorical flourishes that both ornament and obscure deeper linguistic and philosophical commitments. (3) The most pressing of these deep convictions is that politics ought to replace religion as the language of the transcendent.

In the remaining chapters, I want to try a thought experiment in reverse. What might happen if we turned these presuppositions on their heads and simply described what we saw? If Harold John Ockenga or Carl F. H. Henry were aroused from their eternal rest to survey the current evangelical landscape, what would they see? How would they describe it? And what would they do to correct it? The rest of this book unfolds answers to these questions: (1) They would see that large parts of their movement had become worldly. (2) They would use the internal language of heresy to describe that worldliness. (3) They would treat the problem of the loss of transcendence and the substitution of politics as a grave spiritual malady that requires spiritual medicine—namely, repentance—to cure it.

Where to begin? It is perhaps an obscure place: gnosticism, Arianism, Pelagianism, and Donatism all speak more loudly in our history than Simony. Nevertheless, it is Simony that accurately names the spirit that has possessed so much of our movement.

Over two decades ago, I wrote an article entitled "What is Simony?" for "Ask A Theologian," a column that once graced the pages of *Faith Today Magazine*.[1] The then-editor of the magazine asked me what possible relevance an ecclesiastical crime peculiar to the Middle Ages would have for contemporary evangelicals in Canada. I had to justify the column or it would be spiked. I honestly can't remember how I answered my colleague, but the column did get printed, so I suppose I was convincing. And yet here I am writing not just a column, but a chapter, indeed the lead chapter for a whole book on just the same subject. How well will I acquit myself this time around? Ultimately, that's up to you to decide.

I'm convinced that Simony is no mere ecclesiastical crime peculiar to the Middle Ages. Simony names a disposition or pattern of false thought and practice that has been obstinately embraced at the expense of the truth of the gospel. It is a heresy all too common in many churches that have drunk too deeply from the wells of Western culture.

Simony underlies all kinds of conversations in far too many contemporary churches, ecclesial communities, and parachurch organizations. As I explain in the following chapters, it is *the* pattern that unfolds itself into the other heresies that are named in this book as hallmarks of thinking and behaving in much of late modern North American evangelicalism across the various political and theological spectra. Unless we can name it clearly for the sake of repentance before God (as opposed to standing in judgment over others or receiving the world's acceptance), much of our witness will continue to suffer.

That's a tall claim, I know. I am nevertheless persuaded of its truth, and I hope that by the end of this chapter you'll be sufficiently persuaded too. Substantiating it requires that we find our starting point much earlier than the various corruptions that in part led to and in some places followed the Reformation. Simony does not have its beginnings with the buying and selling of church offices in the high Middle Ages. Its foundations are much earlier.

Simon Magus

A Hollywood screenwriter could make much out of the legends that have come to be associated with Simon Magus, or Simon the Sorcerer. He's fascinating—someone straightforwardly at home in Robert E. Howard's *Conan the Barbarian* pulp novels. In apocryphal tradition and the early Fathers,[2] Simon is the chief opponent of that other Simon, the apostle Peter. With his confidante and paramour, Helen, Simon dogs Peter's itinerant ministry all the way to Rome, preaching another gospel. Not only does he identify himself with the persons of the Trinity, his doctrines eventually coalesce into *the* primordial New Testament heresy: gnosticism, which we'll take up in the next chapter. Of course, with an ego large enough to claim both divine identity and knowledge of the secret truth that had not been revealed to Peter the hapless fisherman, Simon had to come up with quite a bag of tricks. Even as the apostles worked miracles (like those described in the book of Acts), Simon Magus substantiated his preaching with false signs and wonders, up to and including soaring around on a flying carpet, to the amazement of all who saw him.[3]

Flashy as they are, the miracle legends are not what interest us. Simony has a much more straightforward (and plausible) origin than the legends suggest. Simon's real story opens as the nascent church moves beyond the confines of Jerusalem to surrounding environs. "But you will receive power when the Holy Spirit has come upon you, and you will be my witnesses in Jerusalem, and in all Judea and Samaria, and to the ends of the earth" (Acts 1:8). The risen Lord's prediction—which also abbreviates and outlines the entire book of Acts—is coming true. The Spirit has come (Acts 2); Jerusalem has been evangelized (Acts 2–6); and Saul has begun his evangelistic work, however unwittingly. By condoning the mob murder of Stephen (Acts 7) and persecuting the first believers, Saul drives them from the city and out into the Judean and Samaritan countryside, taking the good news of Jesus with them (Acts 8:1–3). One of these Jerusalem refugees is a man named Philip (Acts 6:5). Pressed to flee his home by Stephen's stoning, Philip finds himself in Samaria (Acts 8:4), where he announces the apostolic kerygma: that Jesus, whom the Jewish leaders had condemned and the Romans crucified, had in fact risen bodily from the dead and been exalted by God as Lord and

Christ. Mighty exorcisms and other healings then confirmed this simple truth: Jesus reigns, and it's time to bow the knee to him. And it worked. The Samaritans were converted.

Enter Simon. Where his practice of magic once "amazed" the people (Acts 8:9), he is now in the position of eagerly listening to and watching the new teachers who were both like and unlike him. The comparison is apt. Here's why: shock and awe attract crowds, and when one attraction meets competition, the crowds will go to whoever has the better show. Philip, it seems, had poached Simon's audience by performing better miracles and preaching a better message. Presumably, Simon wanted to find out where his followers (and income) had gone, so he searched Philip out. And what did he find? Where Simon had previously compelled people to attend to his words because of his mighty magic (Acts 8:11), the Samaritans saw Philip's mighty acts, believed Philip's message, and were baptized. Simon's stage show could no longer draw. With neither audience nor income, what was the erstwhile magician to do? The text summarizes his actions plainly: Simon believed, was baptized, and remained with Philip (Acts 9:13). The magician who had "amazed" others was now himself "amazed" at Philip's miraculous ministry and became a part of the new movement. If you can't beat 'em, join 'em.

It's an auspicious beginning! At this stage of Simon's story, Acts offers no indication of anything gone or about to go awry. Simon's conversion was by all accounts genuine. Its pattern was that of every other new believer's turn to Christ: Simon heard the word of Jesus's resurrection and ascension and believed. He was baptized. He thereby publicly submitted to the lordship of the true King by identifying himself as one of his followers. And he didn't shrink into obscurity or idiosyncrasy thereafter. The text says explicitly that Simon remained with Philip. He continued in the community of disciples, identifying with them even as they took him in. By any conceivable metric, Simon had forsaken his magic for the Master. He was a disciple of Jesus and a member of his community. His was a "rock star" conversion.

But eventually, everything unraveled.

When the apostles heard that the Samaritans had accepted the word of God (Acts 8:14), they dispatched Peter and John to assess the situation. It seems that Philip's evangelistic work, while good, was in some way incomplete. For while the Samaritans had indeed been baptized, they had not yet received the Holy Spirit, so Peter and John laid their hands on the new believers to impart this gift. Just what the Samaritan reception of the Spirit looked like is not narrated, but it was obvious to all present that the Spirit in fact fell on them. I think readers are right to suppose that the Spirit's Samaritan arrival resembled the events of Acts 2: winds, miraculous languages, and tongues of fire.

Whatever manifestations accompanied the Spirit's outpouring, they certainly were public, and Simon himself saw the reception and was impressed. And just here is where the first worry emerges for the close reader. The text gives no indication that Simon himself received the Holy Spirit with his fellow Samaritan converts. Indeed, though it is not explicit, it strongly intimates exactly the opposite. Simon did not experience the gift of the Holy Spirit given through the laying on of hands but merely saw it (Acts 8:18). Something isn't quite right. He may well have believed, been baptized, and remained with the community, but at that pivotal moment, Simon is not seen standing (or kneeling) with his fellow believers under the apostles' hands. He is apart and aloof. He is an observer, still in some sense an outsider.

Whether Simon genuinely believed, partly believed, or whether his discipleship was merely pretended from the start, the text does not clearly say. Like the outpouring of the Spirit above, to take a position on the authenticity of Simon's conversion involves textual, theological, and pastoral commitments that distract from the point that needs making. Whether Simon had *really* bowed the knee to Jesus under Philip's preaching or not, the Spirit's outpouring seems to have produced a kind of reversion to form for the old magician. I wonder if his thoughts went something like this: "Philip had mighty works that were better even than mine! Philip could dispatch demons and dispel disease, and that's impressive against what I can manage. But the real power? Now that dynamite showed up with Peter and John!" I don't think that I'm inserting too much into the textual silence here because, when we resume reading, we discover that he who had taken "power of God" as his own nickname (Acts 8:10) wanted in on that apostolic action. "Now when Simon saw that the Spirit was given through the laying on of the apostles' hands, he offered them money, saying, 'Give me this power also, so that anyone on whom I lay my hands may receive the

Holy Spirit'" (Acts 8:18–19). This is not the simple error of the new believer. In attempting to buy the Holy Spirit, Simon is unmasked. His conversion, however wonderful it may have at first appeared, is finally false. His story concludes with a rebuke from the apostolic leader:

> Peter said to him, "May your silver perish with you, because you thought you could obtain the gift of God with money! You have neither part nor lot in this matter, for your heart is not right before God. Repent, therefore, of this wickedness of yours, and pray to the Lord that, if possible, the intent of your heart may be forgiven you. For I see that you are in the gall of bitterness and in the bond of iniquity." And Simon answered, "Pray for me to the Lord, that nothing of what you have said may come upon me." (Acts 8:20–24)

What Philip and indeed the narrator of Acts could not see, Peter could. Simon's conversion, whether from his baptism onward or only ultimately in the end, was inauthentic. In spite of his belief, baptism, and discipleship, Simon was not a true follower of Jesus. Philip, the Samaritan believers, even the narrator and us, the readers, had and have been duped. Peter alone discerns that Simon was merely an observer, hoping either for an angle to get his old audience back or to get in on the new gig, to continue dispensing "power," amazing the crowds, and enriching himself.

Simon's story is ultimately very sad and indeed has been symbolically replayed from the first century to the twenty-first countless times. It is the tale of the "not-quite-convert," someone looking for an angle to advance themselves and trying to fit the gospel of the risen Lord into that agenda. The legends of Simon's divine claims and gnostic pronouncements, the fanciful tales of miracles and gravity-defying hijinks, depending on how they're read, either magnify or distract from this point. In the former case, they rightly name the spiritual excesses that can attend a false conversion. But who cares if you have a magic carpet, cast out demons, heal the sick, or raise the dead if in the end Jesus doesn't know who you are? In the latter, they run the risk of becoming the point. I don't work false miracles or teach false doctrine, therefore I am not guilty of the heresy. We are wise to be alert to the latter and properly introspective with the former. For far from anything so exotic as claiming to be God or magic carpet rides, Simon's sin is dreadfully accessible. In reducing the Holy Spirit to a magical power that could be purchased and dispensed for a fee, Simon shows that his interest in Jesus is finally only self-serving. Simon's sin is, simply, the failure to acknowledge Christ's claim over his world and life, hoping instead to fit Christ into his own self-directed agenda.

Simon's heresy was not so much the content of his teaching—though it was false—as it was his disposition. His portrayal in Acts is the embodiment of the false teacher in 2 Peter 2. He is greedy (2 Pet 2:3), bold and arrogant (2:10), and his teaching is proffered not as a claim upon truth but to part people from their money (2:15). The gospel, and indeed the Holy Spirit, were mere means to the end of Simon getting his audience and his comforts back. Simon's tragic tale warns readers against the reduction of the gospel to a product, the elevation of the preacher to its pitchman, and the goal of evangelism to a full wallet and belly.

Seeing Simony

"She's not selling ordination to unbelievers, so how is what she's doing Simony?" That was the question that was posed to me in the early stages of this book's preparation. It came in the context of my description of a particular action as Simony.

It's a fair question. If, as I hope to show below, there's more to Simony than that, then I have to deal with this textbook definition. If anyone knows Simony at all anymore, they will usually define it not as a heresy but as a medieval crime: the attempt to secure a material advantage, public approval, or personal power through the buying or selling of a spiritual good. And of course, the most obvious example is what was an all-too-common practice in the Middle Ages: a powerful family would seek to increase its influence by placing key members in key ecclesiastical positions, greasing the proper palms all the way up the curial ladder.

Dante, whose *Inferno* is quoted at this chapter's outset, reserves an entire trench in the eighth circle of Hell for Simoniacs, and notably popes! In Canto XIX, Dante and Virgil (his underworld tour guide) encounter a spirit upside down in a hole, whose feet are on fire. The damned soul discloses that he is Pope Nicholas III, and he is furthermore eagerly awaiting his successor, Pope Boniface, who will soon join him in the same fate.[4] For when Boniface arrives, Nicholas will be released from the hole and pushed further down into the pit's cracks. Like all the sinners in the *Inferno*, Nicholas's punishment fits his sin. He and his papal cohort, though thought to be successors of the apostle Peter, are actually successors of Simon Magus. Thus their baptism has in hell become a parody, even as Simon's "miracles" feebly imitated the apostles' mighty works of divine power. Simoniacs like Nicholas are suspended upside down in a perverse font, the holy oil of chrismation serving not to seal them with the Holy Spirit but to set their feet on fire. Rather than save them for an ascent into eternal life, baptism is their initiation into an ever-deepening descent into the second death. The spiritual grace they sold for financial and social gain has become the gateway to their eternal damnation. The new pope replacing the old one in the font and the former being pushed even lower into hell for eternity is an anti–apostolic succession, in which the only mobility is downward. Unlike most of the other sinners in the *Inferno*, Dante regards the Simoniacs without qualification or pity of any sort. The medieval context is illuminative. Dante writes at a time when the pope was a temporal *and* spiritual power—he literally commanded armies and governed territory in addition to shepherding souls from earth to heaven. It was also a time when the pope's spiritual power was perceived to be real, and therefore to oppose it was fraught with natural and supernatural danger. To covet it—as those who purchased Nicholas III's favors did—was to place one's soul in jeopardy, just as to dispense it was.

And the eternal cost was not only levied against corrupt ecclesiastics. It is almost impossible today to imagine Pope Francis excommunicating a temporal ruler—a (Catholic) president or prime minister—for some grievous sin. And while such an action might be the fervent hope of some conservative Catholics today, most find the prospect to be so unlikely as to be laughable. Even more unlikely, even more scorn provoking, would be the image of that president or prime minister showing up shoeless at the Pope's front door in winter, seeking absolution for his sin and readmission to Mother Church. And most ridiculous of all would be the image of Pope Francis leaving the penitent politician outside, barefoot and cold, for three days to make certain his repentance was authentic. And yet, this is exactly what happened to Holy Roman Emperor Henry IV and Pope Gregory the VII at Canossa Castle in 1077, when the sharp disagreement over which power—the temporal or the spiritual—could install a bishop came to its climax. The Pope won, at least on one reading, because of the perception of the reality of his spiritual power. Henry could only deprive a body of its head; Gregory could dispatch someone to perdition.

In a cultural context where spiritual power is perceived this way, it is no wonder that some rash souls would seek to obtain it by nefarious means. And so the sin of Simony took on its obvious visible criminal manifestation, buying and selling church offices or the power to appoint to such offices, or seeking to obtain influence through such offices and so on. In many places around the world, similar activities remain conceivable and (probably) practiced. The easy secularism of Western Europe and North America, in which the story of Henry and Gregory seems so foreign, is simply not found in much of the world. Many Christians in Africa, South Asia, or (at least until recently) Latin America or Ireland would be far more at home with Henry and Gregory and far more clear-eyed about the dynamics involved than we are. As I write, for example, the primates of the Churches of North India and South India are both under criminal investigation for financial corruption, specifically the selling of influence. And if we're honest with ourselves, we can find instances where a very literal form of Simony is not that far away from North American pop-evangelicalism. My uncle would, for a lark, regularly write televangelists with prayer requests and the indication of potential monetary donations. In return, he received vials of specially anointed oil, miraculous handkerchiefs, and other such charlatanry with the promise of more to come if the money flowed. Simony even in its crassest forms is alive and well in many places.

But in the context in which you've picked up this book, is that still the case? Hardly. Or at least, rarely. Modernity has taught us that spiritual power, if it exists at all, is of a different sort. It extends into the natural world only as the authority to persuade. Souls, heaven and hell, salvation and damnation—these are realities that, if they exist at all, do so only in the privacy of our own homes and hearts. They may well motivate us to do good, but they are not as real as the good we do. And yet we are wrong to draw from this new situation the conclusion that, having dispensed with the reality of spiritual power, having framed everything within the finite, we are immune to Simony. It may well be true that in both the church and the wider culture, very few of us take the spiritual power of churches and/or their office holders as seriously as they once did and so don't succumb Simony as a crime. It may well be that none of us would give any weight to the image of President X or Prime Minister Y publicly supplicating Pope Z for absolution. But does that mean we are therefore immune to Simony as a heresy? Is Simony to be identified only with the most literal instantiations thereof and not as an even more insidious pattern of thinking?

Imagined, Immanent, and Buffered

The answer to both questions is no. And both will take some unpacking. To do so, I want to borrow three interrelated concepts from the Canadian Catholic philosopher Charles Taylor: the social imaginary, the immanent frame, and the buffered self. These help us understand why the more traditional, straightforward examples of Simony are more difficult for those of us in highly secularized contexts to grasp, and they enable me to articulate why it nevertheless remains a heresy—and a particularly subtle and therefore virulent one.

Let's start with the first: the social imaginary. The social imaginary is the (mostly unconscious) way we cooperatively construct what counts as "the real world."[5] While speaking of a social imaginary allows us to conceive of a space between the world as we perceive it or make it and the world as it is in itself, it need not require us to obliterate the latter, as a hard social constructivist would have it, nor make us in effect Kantians, trapped inside our own inner universe. As I am using the term, we can still speak of better and worse reads of reality; we can even use the stronger language of truth and falsehood. So leaving the epistemological debate aside, let's aim lower. By social imaginary, I mean (and I think I'm following Taylor here) how we perceive "just the way the world is" when we are busy doing other things.

The social imaginary in which Gregory and Henry operated was one in which spiritual power, while distinguished from temporal power, was nevertheless real. As a result, to be excommunicated from Mother Church was not a metaphorical way of expressing disapproval that had real social consequences. It was a literal cutting off from eternal salvation with both an immediate and an after-death effect. Henry lost the support of German princes and looked forward to a "hot" future. Although he lived five centuries after Gregory and Henry, Martin Luther still lived in that same world—one that was, to borrow from his oft-sung hymn, "with devils filled." Luther's preoccupation with the demonic is well-attested.[6] And again, his language was not a metaphor for something else. In his world, devils really did haunt the forests. I suspect that many more people than most Westerners realize still live in that sort of social imaginary. Indeed, as I read of the return of the silly and superstitious in the demise of organized religion, I'm not so sure we've left it that far behind. But that is to get ahead of ourselves. For now, let's just acknowledge that the world we moderns imagine simply isn't the world from which Simony's most obvious examples continue to be drawn.

What is our world then? Here I return to Taylor: our world may be labelled "the immanent frame."[7] There is no need for Luther's devils; no need for an afterlife to account for anything. The deeper "notions and images" that underlie our social interactions need no longer include any nod to God, the transcendent, the supernatural, or the spiritual. The "just the way the world is" is material all the way down. We may even say it is "practically" atheist. Think, for example of a natural disaster—an earthquake, a tornado, or a hurricane—that produces human suffering. The first question that would have driven a Luther, a Gregory, or a Henry—"who sinned?"—simply isn't asked by most people. And if anyone attempts to draw a connection between so-called natural events and moral depravity, they are quickly dismissed as quacks by even the most conservative Christians.

Thus, in the social imaginary that frames the world entirely within the immanent, the self finally is buffered. It is cut off from and ultimately unaccountable to any moral or spiritual significance outside itself.[8] This works in a number of ways, helpfully elucidated in contrast (once again) to what came before. The self of the previous world was porous; that is, there was no sharp distinction between the inner world of the spirit and the external world of matter. Their interpenetration could be seen in several ways: God could cause an earthquake or heal a disease; devils lurked in the forest causing malaise; meaning lay objectively in things and was not simply assigned by the mind. The self of the modern world is buffered: inner and outer are sharply distinguished and kept independent of each other. The movement of tectonic plates causes earthquakes; God, if God exists, has nothing to do with it. Germs, not devils, cause disease. And humans "make" meaning; we do not find it existing independently of us.

In a social imaginary framed immanently, where selves are buffered against the transcendent, it is immediately understandable why Simony is perceived as a relic. If there is even such a thing as spiritual power, it is completely divorced from temporal power, and any sort of traffic between the two, as implied by the buying and selling of ecclesiastical offices, simply makes no sense. A president or prime minister may beseech a pope for pardon, but the matter is private, having nothing to do with policy. But I'm not sure that this means Simony has gone the way of the dodo. It does mean that Simony looks different than it used to; that it is more subtle, less obvious, and therefore, perhaps, even more dangerous than it once was. Simony as a crime akin to spiritual bribery may no longer exist. Simony as a pattern of thinking—a heresy—continues to thrive.

Simony Today

Let's begin with an observation whose unpopularity makes it no less obvious: even immanently framed, buffered selves are religious in orientation. Human beings remain *homo religiosus* even as organized religion recedes, at least in the West. In the absence of religion, the human drive to worship hasn't dissipated but remains and is redirected. The Christian philosopher Alvin Plantinga puts it this way: "The awareness of God is natural, widespread, and not easy to forget, ignore, or destroy."[9] And one need not be in any way religious in an identifiable sense to recognize that human beings are no more at home than when we are on our knees before something. We are hardwired to worship. And what has happened in the secular age that Taylor has so helpfully summarized is not, as the new atheists once confidently predicted and still hope for, the withering of worship, but a transference of divine objects. The need for God has not gone away, and so the language and action of devotion has been transferred to objects in this world: the climate, the homeland, justice (pick a cause), science, whatever.

I have thought long and hard about naming examples—ones more specific than those to which I gestured above. My editor even suggested trying to find a noninflammatory one as I was putting this chapter together. I failed. Each one that I considered not only illuminated of the heresy of Simony currently at work but also was immediately seen to confirm one side in their biases and to ensure the other side put the book down. At the end of the largely fruitless mental exercise, I found myself wondering whether such a list—even if I attempted to be evenhanded to the point of making sure so called "conservative" and "liberal" issues were equally represented—would only end up making Pharisees of us all.

The examples I came up with are all fraught. They are because of the theological and religious baggage they have been improperly forced to carry. In *The Four Loves*, C. S. Lewis speaks eloquently about the dangers of becoming too attached to *storge* (affection), *philos* (friendship), *eros* (sexual love), and *agape* (self-giving love): "We may give our human loves the unconditional allegiance which we owe only to God. Then they become gods: then they become demons. Then they will destroy us, and also destroy themselves."[10] No doubt we can substitute any of the issues I mentioned above and dozens of others alongside for Lewis's loves. It does not diminish their importance to our common life when we notice that in our current discourse, these political issues have usurped God's place in the temples of our hearts. They have become our gods, so they have also become demonic demanders of sacrifice, like the gods of old.

So instead of causes or hot-button topics, let me try three practices that know no side and are claimed by all. Here's the first: When the Bible is deployed to speak *immediately* to a modern political matter, as though there is absolutely no room for reflection or disagreement, be on the alert for Simony. A great example here is poverty. The Scriptures' call to community responsibility for, to borrow from the prophets' own language, "the widow, the orphan, and the stranger" is unequivocal. Those whom God had blessed with abundance were to ensure that people who fell outside the social safety net provided by extended family and clan ties in Israel and Judah would survive. People who, in the advent of a famine, drought, or war, and lacking a husband, father, or clan, would have had little to no means of support were not to be abandoned but helped. This provides biblically serious Christians a common point of orientation with respect to a whole host of contemporary, pressing political issues. Immigration, welfare reform, climate change, you name it: they all are *indirectly* addressed by the Bible's call for care for the poor and the sharing of covenant blessings. But when someone, whether a preacher or a politician, an activist or lobbyist, insists that *the* biblical response to any of these social problems is theirs, such that those who disagree with them are not only mistaken, but also sinful, and not merely sinful, but wicked, somewhere in a hot corner of hell Simon chuckles. For the Scriptures are being pressed to address a problem of which they know nothing. The Bible is ignorant of refugee crises such as we know them today; it knows nothing of the modern nation state or modern border policy; it knows nothing of the tax code; it certainly knows nothing of ice caps and CO_2 levels. It is entirely possible for believers, whose faith in the Scriptures as the revealed word of God is common and whose biblical concern for the poor of our communities and our world is equally fervent, to come to very different answers regarding how best to address any of these issues in particular. When the Bible is misused to make difficult and complex issues seem easy, it is being used to browbeat faithful people into coming to a solution prematurely. It is deploying the language of faith to secure a position in politics. It is Simony.

In a related way, when the Bible is cherry-picked to bolster a cause held for other reasons—both prior and more important—be on the alert for Simony. Perhaps the most obvious example is the endless debate about human sexuality. From Genesis 1:27 forward, the Bible is well aware of the realities of biological sex and marriage. It is amazing to me just how easily, in the popular Christian arguments over marriage, all sides took for granted that the primary—if not exclusive—purpose of marriage is the sanctification of sexual desire, as though procreation and companionship were somehow lesser or even optional goals. To that shared assumption, Bible verses appropriate to the speakers' own preference were then attached. This expression of sexual desire is licit and therefore ought to be blessed. Or not. And, presumably, whoever has the greater number or better quality of Bible verses wins. But, in popular debates at least, rarely was the question-begging of these sorts of arguments pointed out: Who says the sanctification of sexual desire is the primary, or sole, purpose of marriage? Precious little was written about matters that the Bible considers to be very serious: the protection of women, the procreation and raising of children, the uniqueness of Christian marriage over against other forms from the ancient world, or marriage as a sacrament of Christ's spousal union with the church, and so on. Attention to any of these could have been helpful in reframing the debate for all concerned. But—and here the irony is rich—caring for children, to pick one such issue, just isn't sexy. Not only did evangelicals cherry pick from their Bibles, they did so having already bought into the sexual revolution's number one assumption: that the sexual act can and should be decoupled from the normal result of the sexual act—a baby.[11] The point is not to take any side but to suggest why the debate as commonly construed always fails. As above, the Bible is misused to simplify a complex modern issue, to press-gang the laity, and to demonize those who disagree. It is making the language of faith serve the apparently more important this-worldly language of politics. It is Simony.

A tactic common in both of these examples is, lastly, an example of its own: the wedding of authentic Christian commitment to something other than the baptism of the Holy Spirit. In the story of Philip and Simon, the apostles recognized that the Samaritans were now included in the family of faith not because they suddenly had the correct views about Jewish identity, temple worship, or sacrifice, but because the Holy Spirit had fallen on them in a way that the apostles recognized. The coming of the Spirit to Samaria rather than, say, the fullness of Philip's teaching (which is in no way hereby questioned) is what validated the Samaritans' baptism with water. What ought to be even more striking than Simon's audacity in asking if he could purchase the Spirit's power is that the Spirit seems to have passed him by. Although he was baptized, he was not, in the end, truly converted. He did not receive the Spirit, and the Spirit did not receive him. Simon's influence remains today when the mark of who's "in" or not is adherence to a political position rather than the sacrament of baptism or the confession of faith, whether the creed or something more informal. When a political position guards the doors of the church rather than gospel, that gospel is being treated as a means to a political end. And that is Simony.

In our contemporary context, the temptation far too many evangelical Christians are yielding to is a willingness to purchase political power by promising the idols of our age the language of our own devotion. We have reversed the dynamic of kings and emperors approaching bishops and popes but otherwise left it completely intact. Far too many immanently framed, entirely buffered evangelical Christians have agreed, in spite of their rich interior devotional lives, that political power is the only power that matters. They go on to affirm that, if the faith is to remain relevant in the public square, it will have to purchase a claim on that power. What they have failed to do is count the cost. The cost is high: putting the faith's own language and practice to political service. Thus both from the right and the left, like Simon approaching Peter or Henry approaching Gregory, far too many of us are approaching the high priests of the new post-Christian religions of the West, begging for continued relevance.

When we find ourselves in such a situation, we are wise to remember the words of Sir Thomas More in the play *A Man for All Seasons*. Finally on trial for his refusal to acknowledge Henry VIII's marriage to Anne Boleyn, Thomas is confronted by a witness to his "treason," one Richard Rich. Early in the play, Rich sought favor from More and was denied. Now, freshly dressed in the new trappings of the Solicitor General for Wales, it is clear that Rich's perjured testimony against his erstwhile mentor has been purchased by political promotion. Rich's lies on the witness stand finished, and More's fate now all but determined, Rich shamefacedly walks past the former chancellor, his former friend, who then speaks these words: "For Wales? Why Richard, it profit a man nothing to give his soul for the whole world ... but for Wales!" Unlike Sir Thomas, Richard Rich gained status and (literally) kept his head. But as the future saint More points out, Rich's material gains came at the cost of his soul. History records Rich's continued rise at court (which included testifying against Catholic and Protestant martyrs) to the level of Lord Chancellor under Edward VI: Sir Thomas More's former position. Saint Thomas More now kneels with the martyrs before God's throne. Was it worth it?

That's just the wager many evangelicals face today. Is our prioritizing of politics of whatever variety worth it? Do we hope to be saints or merely rich? When the gospel is sublimated to politics, when the Holy Spirit is offered for sale to a worldly purpose, when what belongs to God is rendered unto Caesar—that is Simony.

Simony's Solution: Prudence

What is Simony's solution? In a word, prudence. Think care and attention; the use of proper caution; deliberation in decision-making; using reason in both self- and community governance. In other words, slow down. We live in an ideologically polarized and fraught environment where the right answer must be affirmed "right now!" (Think, "What do we want? When do we want it?")

This is a radically countercultural position to adopt. But the climate crisis is about to destroy us! Wokeism is going to undo our culture! All sides press in upon us for immediate action and the silencing of dissent. If we are going to avoid the heresy of Simony, Christians of all stripes need to start by saying simply—no. Immediacy is not the route to go.

How do I get out from under the false teaching that says the gospel is a commodity to be priced out for political advantage? The first answer is the cultivation of the godly sorrow that works repentance. We need to camp on that for a little while lest we fall to another of late modern evangelicalism's besetting sins: pragmatism. I suggest behaviors below that will, with God's grace, heal us from the self-inflicted wounds I described above. But we need to be clear: wounds are not sins. While wounds need to be healed, sins need to be forsaken.

They need to be—and this is not too strong a word—killed. Only after repentance can healing, and the practical work that needs doing, begin.

So we start not with tips and strategies but with the story of Jesus's temptation in the wilderness (Matt 4:1–11). Our Lord, having been baptized, on the threshold of his public ministry, is led by the Holy Spirit into the wilderness for a diabolical encounter that casts the rest of his mission. Having refused the temptations to satisfy physical needs (whether his own or humanity's) and to compel assent through miracles, Jesus is faced with the gravest temptation yet:

> Again, the devil took him to a very high mountain and showed him all the kingdoms of the world and their glory. And he said to him, "All these I will give you, if you will fall down and worship me." Then Jesus said to him, "Be gone, Satan! For it is written,
>
> > "'You shall worship the Lord your God
> > and him only shall you serve.'"
>
> Then the devil left him, and behold, angels came and were ministering to him. (Matt 4:8–11)

In all the Gospel accounts, the wilderness battle with Satan is really only about one temptation: that Jesus's mission can be accomplished by any means other than the cross. Jesus is Israel—having been brought through the water, he is taken into the wilderness, and he is tempted to test God, to press upon him for a miracle, and to place his hope in something other than his Father. But where Israel failed, Jesus succeeds.

He is just as much the church, which, having been created by water and blood, now carries on the mission of the Son as his Spirit-enlivened body. And where we fail, again, he succeeds. As our representative and our substitute, he guarantees the success of the mission because he has already accomplished it. So before we get to technique, we fix our eyes on Christ, who, thanks be to God, has already delivered us.

The last temptation for Matthew is the temptation to Simony: to secure the success of the mission by means of politics, to buy into the lie that the redemption of humanity will be won by subduing the kingdoms of the world. The temptation to Simony is neither new nor surprising. And, thank God, it has already been resisted to the very end by the Son of God. Centering ourselves on this—which is simply the gospel—frees us from the all-too-common conviction that getting the technique right will fix everything. If we are to do something, to engage in some kind of course correction, let's begin by acknowledging that this is first and foremost a spiritual rather than a pragmatic matter. It is about cooperating with grace in the sanctification of our souls rather than winning an argument.

With that in mind, let's return to the biblical drama I introduced in the previous chapter: King Hezekiah's negotiations in Isaiah 35 and 2 Kings 18. Like Hezekiah and his advisors, evangelicals (indeed, serious Christians of all kinds) are engaged in negotiating life in an increasingly hostile world, and like Hezekiah, there's no guarantee that the negotiations will end well for us. How ought we to proceed? We need to cultivate prudential judgment. This happens, it seems to me, in three steps.

First, relearn the language "inside the walls." Rod Dreher has written eloquently about the pressing need for Christians to rebuild "thick" communities of faithful practice,[12] and there is no more important practice—especially for those Christians formed in the evangelical wing of Protestantism—than the careful and close reading of the Holy Scriptures. In the words of the Book of Common Prayer's collect for the Second Sunday of Advent, we ought to "read, mark, learn, and inwardly digest them." This has the advantage of requiring nothing novel or esoteric to be added to our devotional lives: merely a return to what was for generations accepted evangelical practice. Exegetically based, expository sermons. Individual and corporate Bible study. Scripture memorization for all ages. None of these things are new; all require a deliberation that seems to me to be lacking more and more among both pastors and laypeople who have discovered more important activities. And yet it is the Scriptures read and proclaimed that give us our language "inside the walls"—that is, the linguistic tools we need to think through how we ought to live in this context, imagine faithful responses to specific situations, and communicate those thoughts and images first with our siblings on the inside, then with other Christians, and eventually to the wider world.

Second, listen to expertise. I already can hear the howls about ideologically compromised "experts," but hear me out. Let's go back to the example of poverty above. If I am immersed in the language of the Scriptures as offering a true description of the world and how I and my community are to be in this world, then I am going to care for the poor. But which poor? And how best to care for them? Here, on the particulars, the Bible is silent. But it is in the particulars that we have to get to work. We might want to jump immediately to the large issue of global poverty and its various, complex, and interrelated causes, where the need for expert advice prior to acting or voting is obvious. Yet even when my focus is trained on the immediate needs in front of me, a panhandler, say (as happened regularly to me when I was in parish ministry in an urban center), I do not always know how best to exhibit proper biblical care. Whether the issue is large or small, whether the expertise is in monetary or foreign policy, mental health or addictions, I have to listen to people whose expertise will help me and my community respond well.

Third, deliberate. Listening to the experts does not mean letting or even demanding that the experts decide for us. Whether global or local, poverty can be investigated and unpacked in any number of ways by any number of experts who will not always agree with each other and whose proposals, though contradictory, will nevertheless seem reasonable. And that's before the challenges that arise uniquely from ideological polarization come in to play. Even when everyone is determined to "play well with others," there is no situation in which we can absolve ourselves of responsibility by simply doing what the experts tell us. If anything, the ideologically fraught nature of expert consultation today requires even more caution, and more deliberation, even as it pushes us to quick responses. Whether in the best of all possible worlds or the worst, there is no avoiding the need to exercise prudence in judgment, and from there to own whatever decisions we make.

Conclusion

Let's go back to the question I tried to answer two decades ago: What is Simony, anyway? Are we any closer now? I think we are. In the medieval era, Simony was rendering unto God, or at least his representatives, what belonged to Caesar in order to gain purchase on Caesar's power. Today the dynamic remains, even as the poles are switched: today Simony is the rendering unto Caesar what belongs to God in order to obtain or retain Caesar's status and approval. And I fear that without repentance and the fruits thereof, the end of our latter-day Simoniacs will be the same as the poor popes of Canto XIX. Having sold the treasures of the gospel, the trumpet will indeed sound for them, and their end will be destruction. Succumbing to this temptation does have serious—eternally serious—consequences.

Simony is but the beginning. Heresies, like demons, are never content to remain alone. Once churches surrender to the siren call of political power, their gospel becomes an eccentric hobby, a mere add-on to an otherwise happy life (gnosticism), their ethics to self-improvement (Arianism), their mission to social action (Pelagianism), and their self-righteousness obvious (Donatism). That is the rest of the story.

Chapter 3

GNOSTICISM

Apologetics as Accommodation

These men are Christians not only in the sense
that they count themselves believers in the Lord
but also in the sense that they seek to maintain
community with all other believers. Yet they seem
equally at home in the community of culture. They
feel no great tension between church and world, the
social laws and the Gospel, the workings of divine
grace and human effort, the ethics of salvation
and the ethics of social conservation or progress.

H. Richard Niebuhr, *Christ and Culture*

T he last chapter suggested that significant chunks of the evangelical movement in North America are, wittingly or not, participating in the heresy of Simony. In the face of demographic decline, they have begun to render unto Caesar what belongs to God in order to obtain or retain Caesar's status and approval. Instead of secular rulers seeking the influence of ecclesiastics—the Simony of the medieval era—today we find Christian leaders all too ready to prostitute the gospel for the sake of influence. The positions may be reversed; the dynamic is the same. Far from being relegated to the moldy corners of medieval history, Simony remains alive and well, and it is a particular temptation for North American evangelicals seeking to retain social and political capital.

While I hope this suggestion was persuasive, the previous chapter was not an argument. It did not move from accepted premises to a conclusion using a logically valid form, nor did it assemble and interpret scads of concrete data from church history or the sociology of religion. Rather, it was an invitation to *see* things in a particular way. I took it as obvious that our movement is significantly hampered by the notion that everything is now politics and politics is everything, and, equally obvious, the incessant, increasingly shrill demand to find the right solution to a political problem that drowns out our Lord's call to take up the cross. I offered an account of why this might be the case: because we have rendered unto Caesar what belongs to God, Caesar has, in fact, become god, and politics has become the end of our common life (goal or destruction? The ambiguity is deliberate).

If Caesar has taken the role rightly reserved for God, this dynamic ought to be observable in other areas of evangelical life. Heresies, like demons, don't come to inhabit houses all by themselves. In this chapter, then, we'll take the descriptive exercise further. Whereas evangelicals were once derided for their sectarianism, for drawing too sharp a distinction between church and world, that gap has been narrowing for the last thirty years or so. Oh sure, we still believe in Jesus. But the Jesus we believe in is one entirely at home with us and with our world, and we'll be glad to tell you why. The focus of our new mission is not souls in need of saving, but those poor benighted Christians who consistently fail to get with the program. In addition to Simoniacs, we have become gnostics.

Gnosticism in the Bible

Like the charge of Simony, this one is not immediately obvious. Just as no evangelical today is trying to buy the Holy Spirit like Simon did in Acts 9, or purchasing an episcopacy for his teenage son like a Florentine magistrate, no evangelical is teaching that the *pleroma* is full of *aeons*, the greatest of whom is named Christ. So we'll need to meander a little to establish the charge.

Once again, however, we begin with the Bible. In Acts 9, Simon tried to buy the Holy Spirit. He thought spiritual realities were available for purchase and were at the disposal of the apostles. Outside Scripture, Simon is also remembered as the founder of gnosticism.[1] Whether or not that is the case, it's certainly true that gnosticism finds its way into the pages of the New Testament. Where Simon's story is straightforward, however, gnosticism lurks in the shadows. Indeed, it skulks behind some of the most beautiful poetry of the New Testament. Consider the climax of John's masterful rewriting of Genesis 1: "And the Word became flesh and dwelt among us, and we have seen his glory, glory as of the only Son from the Father, full of grace and truth" (John 1:14).

John insists that the Logos, who was with God in the beginning—indeed, who was God (John 1:1–4)—could and did take up flesh. This was a shot across the bow to those Christians (and others) who believed that such a thing was impossible. John's use of the Old Testament motifs of tabernacle[2] and glory emphasizes that God the Logos was rendered gloriously visible in the entirely human flesh of Jesus of Nazareth. This Word was not only heard but seen and even handled (1 John 1:1), and any teacher who says otherwise does not, as far as John is concerned, have apostolic validation or authority. Only those teachers who confess that Jesus came in the flesh are animated by the Spirit; those who deny it are animated by the spirit of antichrist. While gnostic groups—whether Christian or pagan—may be the heretics challenged by other parts of the New Testament (Colossians, for example), there is no doubt that their great New Testament opponent was the Fourth Evangelist and the author of 1 John.

Who Were the Gnostics?

Like Peter, who had Simon Magus riding on his coattails, early Christian tradition tells us that John had his own personal gnostic nemesis in Ephesus, where the apostle lived. His name was Cerinthus. Indeed, Irenaeus of Lyons suggests that John's Gospel was penned explicitly to refute Cerinthus's teaching.[3] Far from a mere battle of ideas, however, the rivalry between John and Cerinthus mimicked Peter and Simon's insofar as it was deeply personal. Irenaeus recounts:

> There are also those who heard from him [Polycarp] that John, the disciple of the Lord, going to bathe at Ephesus, and perceiving Cerinthus within, rushed out of the bath-house without bathing, exclaiming, "Let us flee, lest even the bath-house fall down, because Cerinthus, the enemy of the truth, is within."[4]

John's point, it seems, is that those who departed from the "rule of truth"[5] even now stood under threat of imminent divine judgment. John's Gospel was written not to persuade Cerinthus but to preserve John's flock. Cerinthus and other false teachers were to be avoided at all costs.

Unlike the stories surrounding Simon Magus and Peter, those starring Cerinthus and John have a surer historical footing. Irenaeus himself is at pains to insist that he heard the bathhouse story from Polycarp, who himself heard it from the Beloved Disciple. (Indeed, historical connection is one of the keys to Irenaean antignostic arguments.) Simon himself may well have founded a gnostic school; on the other hand, he may be a literary cypher under which several teachers and/or systems of thought have been subsumed.[6] Basilides, Saturninus, and Valentinus are known founders of other gnostic-Christian schools, though their thought is preserved mostly in the writings of their catholic opponents.[7]

Furthermore, gnosticism was not an exclusively Christian or even especially a Christian phenomenon. Jewish, Iranian, and Syrian gnosticisms flourished before and alongside it.[8] Rather than naming one object, then, gnosticism is best thought of as an umbrella term, one that highlights a series of family resemblances across antiquarian religion, both Christian and otherwise.[9] When it comes to its teachings, what follows ought to be read in the broadest of terms.

Christian gnosticism is a "salvation religion" from top to bottom, about the transition of the human spirit from the lower world of matter to the higher world of spirit. It hinges on two interrelated dualisms. The first sunders God from the Creator. God is pure spirit, and from God emanates the aeons, who are the divine attributes personified in a series of male and female pairs. Together, these constitute what we might call the divine realm, the "pleroma." Posited against God is the Creator (the "demiurge," or Craftsman), who made everything else that is not divine. Although gnostic teachers might have disagreed among themselves about the origins of the lesser god, whether he was an intermediary gone wrong or an eternally existent, inferior "less-than-God," they were certain this god was the source of the visible universe and was also the God of the Jews and an enemy of the true Supreme Being.

The second dualism is also now obvious. God is the source of all that is spirit and good or noble; the demiurge, on the other hand, accounts for matter, which is not so much evil as it is ignoble or base. An intriguing cosmology and metaphysics, to be sure, heavily indebted to Platonic and Neoplatonic thought, Jewish apocalypticism, and Pythagorean mysticism, among other sources. But the cosmology was not the point. Jaroslav Pelikan's observation remains apt: this was all about "dealing with the human predicament."[10]

What is that predicament? The mythology varies from school to school, but the theme is constant: human beings are hybrids. Having once lived among the aeons, they fell from their place of privilege and became entrapped or even entombed in material bodies. Salvation was conceived as the spirit's liberation from base matter at death to return to its true, spiritual state. The understanding of human beings as spirit/matter hybrids, and of salvation as leaving the body behind at death, was not invented by Christian gnostics, their predecessors, or their contemporaries. It finds classical expression in Plato's allegory of the charioteer in the *Phaedrus*. It is as old as the Upanishads (c. 1000 BC). In describing the fall and salvation of humanity in these sorts of ways, the Christian gnostics were anything but original. They were swimming in the thought-ocean of their day, entirely at home.

What made Christian gnostics unique was, simply, Jesus the Savior. Where early Christian thinkers—Justin Martyr, Irenaeus, Hippolytus, and others—were beginning to reflect on the person and work of Jesus in ways that would culminate two centuries later in the doctrines of the Trinity and the hypostatic union, the gnostics moved in a different direction, articulating a vision of Christ that fit better with a dynamic already well entrenched in their thought world. Rather than the Son of Mary, the divine Christ was an emissary from the aeons. Perhaps he only appeared to be a man (a subheresy that has been given its own name: Docetism, from *dokeo*, "to appear"). Perhaps he was a spirit being who possessed the body of the man Jesus of Nazareth from his baptism. Either way, he certainly was not born of Mary, contaminated by her matter. Where the apostolic fathers, apologists, and other early theologians stressed the reality of Mary's motherhood at every turn, for the gnostics, Jesus was at most light who passed through Mary as light through a window or as water through a hose. If the idea that a spiritual savior could become human was inconceivable, the idea that he would do so through conception and birth was, literally, disgusting.

The emphasis then fell not on the person or passion of Christ but on his teachings, which disclosed the secret truths and rituals through which spirits could be set free from their bodily tombs at death. Not, of course, those teachings preserved in the rule of truth, the bishops, and the documents that would become the four Gospels. Rather, Christian gnostics offered secret teachings passed from Jesus to an elect few, and from them to the spiritual elite of the current day. Following those teachings could result in opposite lifestyles: either extreme asceticism to mortify corrupt bodily desires and free the spirit, or extreme license because the body, being a temporary house meant only for destruction, could not contaminate the spirit it contained. The cross of Christ did not save; it revealed the mystery of human destiny.[11] And it was certain that the Savior did not suffer! The notion that the Son of God should suffer and die made as little sense as that he should be born. Salvation was found not in the events of incarnation and atonement themselves but in the truths they revealed. Salvation was about the acquisition and implementation of secret knowledge: hence the name, gnosticism.

Gnostic Apologists

What are we to make of this strange collection of esoteric teachings? Outside a New Age bookstore, the specifics are not widely held by anyone today. They are too other-worldly, too immaterial for our material era. Whether or not a world beyond our senses is the real world—well, who really debates that outside university classrooms full of classics or philosophy majors? And even there it's a minority position. Simply to grasp Plato's insistence that the world of ideas is real and eternal while the world of the senses is at best a malleable copy and at worst an illusion requires a mental leap akin to religious conversion for almost all of us, including Christians, or at least those who live in the secular West.[12]

Nevertheless, there are significant parallels between the days of the Christian gnostics and the late modern West. Perhaps most obvious is the instrumentalization of matter, especially the body. We may well have relinquished any belief in the spirit. Even if we give mention to it weekly, how does that belief differentiate believers from nonbelievers in everyday life? Moreover, we have come around to the notion that the material world is malleable, illusory, and even base. Nothing has meaning in itself; meaning is not discovered. Meaning, rather, is forced upon matter by what we do with it. Human beings are, in the sociological shorthand of today, meaning-makers. In the most extreme example, my body is not me; instead, it is the canvas I adorn or alter to display the real, inner me. Of course, the inner me is not a spirit or soul. It is simply my ultimately biologically generated desires. My body has no inherent logic, no built-in significance, no innate truth to impart to my desires or by which they might be understood and disciplined. My desire for self-construction and self-actualization trumps all. "I desire, therefore I am" is not too strong a way to put it. My body is the vehicle through which I display my true self to the world. Examples range from the trivial, such as fashion and tattoos, to the grave, such as sex reassignment surgeries and other forms of self- and surgical mutilation.[13]

Those parallels are worth deep thought and have been and are being considered by others far more capable than I am. My aim is lower. Let us grant both the surface implausibility of ancient gnostic beliefs for a contemporary Western audience and the deeper (and deeply disconcerting) similarities. Somewhere in between is the recognition that the Christian gnostics were entirely wedded to the spirit of their age, and accordingly were widowed in the ages that followed. They were at home in their world. They held beliefs that pretty well everyone, apart from an ancient Cynic or two, would have affirmed. They were well-read and conversant with the science of their day. Were we to take up an English translation of a gnostic document from the Nag Hammadi library, such as *The Gospel of Truth*, or were we to read the summaries of the beliefs of gnostic schools found in Hippolytus and Irenaeus, we would be confused. We would not comprehend the truly bizarre vocabulary of aeons in the pleroma, intermediate archons, the demiurge who fashioned the material universe. Obviously incredible by today's knowledge, not only would we not believe it, but we might also be unable to understand how people of that day could have believed it either. And there we would make a fundamental error.

The gnostic Christians whose beliefs I summarized above may well have been secretive about their rituals, but their beliefs were surprisingly mainstream. We read them wrongly if we read them as masters of esoterica. They were Christians in some sense. They believed that they had encountered in Jesus the Savior of the world. And they took it upon themselves to minimize the distance between Jesus and their world as much as possible. If we are to understand just how ancient gnostics help us see how at least parts of evangelicalism have gone off the rails, we need to understand them as (finally heretical) Christian apologists.

When we think of apologists for the first Christian generations, we usually think of Justin Martyr, or perhaps Tertullian. We think of those who took up the pen against great minds of the day, doing battle with ideas. Or we remember those who pled with magistrates and emperors to make the case that the new faith was not irrational and that Christians posed no threat to the security of the Roman Empire. They defended Christian faith to philosophers and politicians for two entirely laudable goals: they hoped to show its plausibility or its intellectual heft, and by so doing they wished to make the majority culture less suspicious of the new faith. Justin, for example, used the language of the *logos* to argue that the light that enlightened every man had indeed enlightened the greatest minds of pagan antiquity, so that what had become incarnate in Christ fulfilled their deepest longings. And while he acknowledged that Christian ritual might be different than pagan ritual, it was not what its critics thought. If Christian citizens could not participate in the imperial cult, they nevertheless prayed for the emperor regularly and were anything but seditious.[14]

It is very difficult to show that the aims, if not the content, of the works of Valentinus, Basilides, Saturninus, and the rest were different. By adopting the metaphysics of the day entirely, by removing all hints of Jewish sectarianism, and by attempting to articulate a Christ-centered understanding of salvation within them, the gnostics were committed to making Christian claims plausible to their audience. On their reading of reality and of salvation, Christianity was little different than the mystery religions of Mithras or Osiris or innumerable others with their own secretive rituals and paths to enlightenment. The gnostic version of Christianity may well be novel—in some sense, Jesus stands among but is not reducible to his competitors—but in the most important way, the gospel retold a tale as old as time: Christ claimed no loyalty over the body, but only over the spirit. Fealty to Christ therefore did not necessarily mean failing to do one's duty to the emperor. After all, what's a pinch of incense? Such a trifle cannot contaminate the really real. This was an "association of the enlightened who could live in a culture as those who sought a destiny beyond it, but who were not in strife with it."[15]

If both the apologists and the gnostics were defenders of Christianity, or at least some version of it, what set them apart? Those led by Justin and Tertullian thought the apostolic faith could be understood, at least enough for their pagan readers to grasp that adherents to the new faith did not deserve persecution. They nevertheless recognized that Christian faith was *new*. It was neither simply a Jewish sect, and therefore covered by the imperial protections extended to its parent faith, nor a reiteration of the familiar dualistic myth that underlay so much of pagan antiquity. If the persecution of Christian faith was wrong, its radical demands still had to be reckoned with. For the apologists, Christ called the pagan world to conversion. And that is exactly what their gnostic contemporaries denied. For the Christian gnostics, the world needed no conversion. Christian faith was entirely compatible with the world as it was. It was always already unconditionally accepted. If the apologists wanted to end the persecutions by converting the world, the gnostics wanted to end the persecutions by converting the church.

The tactic is easily seen in their preening elitism: they did not found churches, they founded schools. They were heirs to the "secret knowledge" that Christ withheld from the Twelve. With the gnosis bestowed instead upon their own hidden enlightened masters, they alone knew the real meaning of the rituals that the apostolically dependent/descendent Catholics, in their poor benighted naivete, could only gesture at. Where the church was enraptured by the merely symbolic, they had encountered that to which the symbols pointed: Ultimate Reality. Like the king in the South Asian folktale of the elephant and the blind men, they could see entirely what the blind men could only partially sense.[16] Bishops and the apostles who trained and sent them were objects of pity, if not scorn.[17]

Evangelical Gnostics?

In his classic work, *Evangelicalism in Modern Britain*, historian David Bebbington offers a fourfold definition of the evangelical movement in Britain: conversionism (the new birth as a definable, dateable event in the believer's life), biblicism (the expectation that the Bible speaks to contemporary life and provides an absolute standard for ethics), activism (evangelicals have social reform in their DNA), and evangelism (a willingness to spread the gospel).[18] Now known as the Bebbington Quadrilateral, it has become an object of fascination, criticism, and development among historians. It remains useful as a point of orientation for evangelical self-understanding. Even in our inward focus on religious experience and the centrality of the Bible, we are outward facing: we want others to experience the new birth too, and we hope to see whole societies formed by the gospel for the common good. Even in our contemplation we have always been outward facing. And that means we are perennially concerned with the intertwined tasks of apologetics and relevance. Take the former first. In the publishing world, apologetics is a burgeoning field that runs from the academic to the popular, the careful and well-researched to the shabby. Even the current move *against* apologetics among some leftward leaning evangelicals (at least as traditionally understood and conducted) is an essentially apologetic move. It is about commending authentic Christian faith to people put off by inauthentic expressions. One may wonder whether the works make it to the intended audience—the thoughtful, inquiring unbeliever—or even whether it is good that they sometimes do. But whatever the case, evangelicals make natural apologists because defending the faith is in our DNA.

But for evangelicals, removing obstacles, intellectual or otherwise, is simply not enough. We want to commend the faith to those who do not yet share it. Our commitment to social action rests on the assumption that biblical faith, or at least a life lived in congruence with biblical norms, is not just good for *us*. It's good for the whole. Our commitment to evangelism means we want people to hear the good news of Jesus in a language they understand, both literally and metaphorically. For the sake of the gospel, we want to minimize the distance between the gospel and the world as much as possible. We want to exploit the commensurability of the language inside the walls with the language outside the walls. We want to translate as much as possible. We want to *be relevant*. In my lifetime, the evangelical pastor went from a blue suit, red tie, older, established authority figure, making pronouncements from a big Bible on a pulpit, to a youngish, bearded, plaid shirt-and-skinny jeans-wearing hipster with a hint of a tattoo at the left sleeve, scrolling through an iPad on a plexiglass podium (if there is a podium at all). The former stood in an obvious church, the latter in a concert venue or multipurpose room. The former belonged to an obvious church like First Baptist Church or Mount Zion Wesleyan Church. The latter fronts The Community, The Bridge, The Soul Smiths—congregations with names that are spiritually suggestive but seem to obscure that they are, in fact, still churches. That's a *massive* amount of change, and not in appearance only. But both pastors look the way they do, worship in the way they do from where they do, and curate their presentation in large part for the sake of relevance. The medium is malleable; the message is not. Once one appearance is no longer relevant, it is easily shed for another. We want to bring the gospel to people in a winsome and understandable way. Like apologetics, relevance is close to the heart of who we are.

For most of its history, evangelicalism has conceived itself as a renewal movement within Christendom with a well-defined sense of otherness—what Niebuhr would call "sectarianism." That is, we had a clear if sometimes idiosyncratic sense of boundaries that marked our community as different from the world. But, oddly enough, it was a difference that persisted "inside the walls" (to recall the image of an earlier chapter). In our desire to defend the faith and to be relevant in our presentation, outside genuinely crosscultural encounters on what was once called "the foreign mission field," we were talking to at least semiformed Christians. Whether their commitment to Christian faith was explicit, and whether their *rejection* of Christian faith was explicit, the objects of evangelicalism's efforts had been formed in a Christian culture, were intuitively or unconsciously aware of Christian symbols, and effectively lived in a Christian thought and life universe—a Christian social imaginary. But then things changed.

First, evangelicals lost their otherness. Henry, Graham, Ockenga, and other leaders of the then "neoevangelical" movement thought that the community could both maintain its distinctives and engage the wider culture. They would forsake the strict separationism of their fundamentalist forebears but would not thereby lose their saltiness (Matt 5:13). In the intervening years, however, evangelicalism began to transcend its blue-collar background. The three decades from the seventies to the nineties saw the establishment of an evangelical elite, who, even if we (yes, I include myself) did not distinguish ourselves in fields outside biblical studies and theology, or if none of us could really claim the title "public intellectual" (this was Noll's point in *The Scandal of the Evangelical Mind*), we at least began to hold our own in these fields. We got postgraduate degrees from Oxbridge and Yale and St. Andrews. We replaced our teachers at evangelical flagship schools like Trinity Evangelical Divinity School, Wycliffe College, Gordon-Conwell, and Wheaton. We even managed to secure appointments to the very universities that gave us our graduate degrees. Heck, we even started to write speeches for American presidents and find our words in the New York Times. By 1995 or so, it looked like we had made it.

From here on, so we hoped, we would defend the faith winsomely (relevant apologetics) from the inside of elite institutions and culture. In those heady days, there was even talk of a Roman Catholic/evangelical alliance that would replace the by now moribund mainline Protestantism and would reset the moral tone for public life.[19] But it was not to be. Even as evangelicalism entered the mainstream, the mainstream began deliberately to apostatize. In the two decades following 9/11, North American culture makers moved from nominally churched to dechurched to unchurched to antichurch with breathtaking speed. In 2005, sociologists Christian Smith and Melinda Lundquist Denton coined the term "Moral Therapeutic Deism" to name the common faith of America's youth.[20] In this religion, God was remote and largely uninvolved in one's life (deism) but was available when needed to raise one's self-esteem or supply a need (therapeutic); its adherents were, above all else, nice (moralistic). Moral Therapeutic Deism found expression across the churches and faith communities of America. According to Smith's data, Jewish and Christian, Protestant and Catholic, evangelical and mainline young people were Moral Therapeutic Deists before anything else.

Within a decade, cultural observers took note that the subliminal, shared Moral Therapeutic Deism had begun to morph with the rise of a generation of young people who had disaffiliated from their parents' and grandparents' churches: the nones.[21] For the most part, the nones were not atheists. They were not even agnostics. Some continued to identify as Christians. They were "spiritual but not religious." They "loved Jesus, but not the church." And with no public Christian culture to keep them coming back to church, they didn't. In the intervening decade, the nones had children. And with respect to the faith of this next generation, to quote sociologist Stephen Bullivant, "from nothing comes nothing."[22] In the space of three decades, we've moved culturally from "Christian" to "no longer Christian" to the now-emerging "never was." Another sociologist, Arthur E. Farnsely II, helpfully (and hopefully) points out that Bullivant's story is a very white one. It simply does not take into consideration or apply to the growth in religious observance among immigrant communities in Britain and America.[23] But if Farnsely rightly narrows the scope of Bullivant's research, he does not undermine it. While there is another, more optimistic story to be told from the margins, North American elite post-Christian culture and its institutions remain predominantly white, for all its posturing about diversity.

So it was that evangelical elites found ourselves sitting at the cultural table just as the culture began to slough off the last of its visible Christian commitments. When we arrived in 1995, we could conceivably continue our strategies of apologetics and relevance because even then there was enough of a shared Christian worldview to enable a common conversation. It was still all talk "inside the walls." But that didn't last long. We did not and do not have any sort of "social teaching" because, as a renewal movement within (Protestant) Christendom, we never had to develop one. Further, outside the limited sphere of influence of a coalition like Evangelicals and Catholics Together, we have not tried to adopt or adapt Catholic social teaching, even as our place at the table has become more precarious.

Instead, we chose the route of Simony. If we did not agree with our post-Christian interlocutors that politics was the only thing, we certainly were willing to say it's the most important. After all, we've always been all about relevance. The evidence? On every social political debate, evangelicals have bifurcated completely across the left-right political axis and put the for-sale sign on the treasures of the church for whatever politician needed us most. The French have a saying: *les extrêmes se touchent*, or "the extremes touch." When evangelicals surrendered to politics, when we became willing to sell our language to those outside the walls for the sake of cultural influence, when we bowed the knee to the postmodern Baal, we did it across the movement. Evangelicals on the right are as indictable as evangelicals on the left.

Not only did we become Simoniacs, but we also thereby became gnostics. Like them, we sought to bring Jesus to a culture by closing the gap between the two as much as possible. Like them, we ended up adopting the culture, losing Jesus, and scorning our own piety. Essentially, we repeated the apologetic strategy undertaken in 1799 by Friedrich Schleiermacher in his classic, *On Religion: Speeches to Its Cultured Despisers.*[24] Faced with the end of the Enlightenment and the collapse of Protestant confessionalism, Schleiermacher sought to defend Christian faith to the Romantics, whom he called "cultured despisers," the nones of his day. He insisted that while the doctrines of institutional Christian faith varied across time and place, the essence of religion remained unaltered. The waning of Protestant rationalism under the advent of modern criticism therefore posed no threat to Christians. Christianity's doctrines and miracles do not begin to encapsulate the feeling of absolute dependence on God aroused in our hearts by the Redeemer. A brilliant apologetic strategy: it effectively created liberal Protestantism. But the cost was high: Romanticism embraced, the Jesus of the Scriptures and the church forsaken, and Schleiermacher's own Pietist heritage dismissed. Schleiermacher sought to defend Christian faith but instead became a cultured despiser himself.

The contemporary American evangelical Jesus, whether of the right or the left, bears little resemblance to the Jesus of the Bible. He is the Jesus who underwrites our political causes and questions only those of our opponents. For every Russell Moore who wonders aloud how some evangelicals can vote for a foul-mouthed, thrice-married, casino and strip-club owner with apparent ease,[25] there is a David P. Gushee calling for—indeed seeming to take a disturbing glee in—the power of the state to silence any evangelical dissent to the LGBTQ+ agenda.[26]

What would Jesus do? Depends on the Jesus. He is entirely captive to the political needs of social conservation or social progress. Whether claimed by the evangelical right or left, the Lord is entirely the "Christ of culture" for far too many. With the gap between Christ and culture obliterated, apologetics and even evangelism is no longer directed at the culture but at those evangelicals who don't get with the program. The culture doesn't need to be converted; other Christians do.

Gnosticism's Solution: Realism

If repentance from Simony looks like turning toward prudence, what does forsaking gnosticism look like? Perhaps it's not surprising that in this case, repentance looks like an embrace of realism.

First, repentance means embracing realism with respect to the natural world. This realism, in turn, rests on two ultimately theological assumptions. First, the world outside our minds exists and is ordered in such a way that it can be known. Second, our minds, when they are functioning properly, can know it. That the world outside our minds exists independently of us (or at least other minds) is, for now anyway, uncontroversial.[27] Perhaps more controversial is the claim that our minds are ordered not just to discover what "works," or whatever enables us to survive, but what actually *is* the case. There is no reason discovered in evolutionary biology showing why this should be true. And yet, the fact that evolutionary biology exists is testament that it is true. Whether or not these assumptions become more embattled in the future remains to be seen. Either way, they are theological corollaries of the Christian doctrine of creation: that God out of an abundance of love created all that is not God; that this creation bears an imprint of divine rationality and so can be known; and that human minds, when functioning properly, can know truths about it.

The implication is that repenting of gnosticism means defending the natural sciences and granting their practitioners the freedom they need to do their proper work. Perhaps the most challenging responsibility of believers here is the refusal to end inquiry prematurely. As an always-ongoing investigation into the natural world, scientific inquiry is never done. It is always open to refinement and revision and sometimes even replacement. Nazis and Stalinists are infamously remembered and rightly castigated for their willingness, even enthusiasm, to colonize science according to their ideologies. On the procrustean beds of Aryan purity or scientific socialism, the findings of the natural sciences were stretched or lopped off according to predetermined conclusions. The sublimation of truth-seeking to ideological conformity, however, is not peculiar to the totalitarianisms of the first half of the twentieth century. The Covid pandemic, now thankfully receding as I write, demonstrated that both political expedience and naked know-nothing populism could expand or restrict the science for their own ends.[28] Precious few voices sought a route between this Scylla and Charybdis, and even fewer listened. On this matter, evangelicals were no more or less guilty than others. No doubt these are challenging days, but the way forward for believers in Jesus is clear, if unpopular, for both ends of the spectrum: "trust the science" must flow hand in hand with "put not your trust in princes" (Ps 146:3). The deep structures on which natural scientific method rests and depends are not simply theological but are in fact Christian. Accordingly, there is or ought to be a deep affinity between robust Christian faith and the pursuit of truth in the natural sciences.[29]

Perhaps my next claim will be more challenging: repentance of gnosticism means embracing moral realism, the conviction that one can derive an *ought* from an *is,* and indeed that human cultures have done so consistently across time and geography. Moral realism is what C. S. Lewis called "the Tao" in *The Abolition of Man*. As he puts it, "I shall henceforth refer to for brevity simply as 'the Tao.' ... It is the doctrine of objective value, the belief that certain attitudes are really true, and others really false, to the kind of thing the universe is and the kind of things we are."[30] Lewis's Tao, simply, is the law of God written on the fabric of the universe and in every human heart. We evangelicals are perhaps more comfortable with a divine command theory of morality, summed up in Billy Graham's famous prefix, "The Bible says ... " And yet Psalm 19 and Romans 1:18–32 together declare the deep affinity between God's good creation and God's law. We shouldn't be surprised when we find broad areas of agreement in morality with people of other faiths or none. And when we do diverge, our first and best apologetic strategy is to appeal to the law of nature.

To leave the matter here, however, is insufficient, if not overly optimistic. Were a rejection of gnosticism to involve merely an embrace of natural and moral realism, the move would be, ironically enough, from ignorance to enlightenment through education. It would be gnostic to the core. What makes such an account sub-Christian is that it has yet to consider the reality of human sinfulness. For despite the deep affinity between the rationality of the universe and the rationality of our minds, in spite of the transcultural, cross-historical reality of the moral law within us, we neither know nor do as we ought. We're not simply finite and therefore ignorant. We're also sinners who willfully embrace blindness. In the words of the prayer of confession, "We have left undone those things which we ought to have done, and we have done those things which we ought not to have done, and there is no health in us."[31]

So a third level of realism ought to form our repentance: biblical realism. The term was coined by Dutch missiologist and theologian Hendrik Kraemer in his 1938 classic, *The Christian Message in a Non-Christian World*.[32] Kraemer uses this term to express the conviction that the great story of God's search for humanity as narrated in the Bible simply is the truth. Writing at a time when competing ideologies were on the precipice, about to plunge the world into the worst global conflict it had ever seen, Kraemer called for Christian believers to recover a sense of confidence in the Christian message, which in turn would enable them to articulate a realistic perspective on human beings, the world, and—in his immediate context— the empirical religions, including empirical (that is, institutional) Christianity. If he is remembered at all, Kraemer is often dismissed as a Barthian, or worse, a fundamentalist. But his point is worth serious consideration.[33] The biblical story cannot be adapted and adopted into modernity. It must out-narrate, transform, indeed convert and annihilate modernity. And this is precisely what gnostic evangelicals have forgotten. We have reduced the Scriptures to a handbook that offers wisdom to otherwise happy lives. But the Bible is not a handbook, and its purpose is not to produce a happy, well-adjusted life. Its purpose is to absorb the world, to tell the truth about it, and to call it and us to repentance.

We can, finally, sharpen biblical realism further for a fourth level: repentance of gnosticism means an embrace of christological realism. That is, the Scriptures testify about Jesus Christ, and the Christ given to us by the Scriptures is the real Jesus. The ease with which Jesus can be adopted into this or that political cause by late modern evangelicals is easily observed; what is not so easily observed, but is nevertheless present, is the ease with which all involved wrench the Jesus of the Gospels out of his literary-theological context—namely, the Old Testament. The temptation to turn the Scriptures into a wax nose persists—to co-opt Jesus into a program we believe for other, prior reasons. The only way to resist that temptation, it seems to me, is to remember that the Scriptures to which Jesus and Paul appealed, the Scriptures that testify to Christ, are gathered together under the name, "The Old Testament."

On this some ground must be given to the gnostics, at least at the level of perception. The Old Testament is, for us as for the ancient gnostics, a foreign world, a world whose preoccupation with blood and other bodily fluids can be gross. And yet, the Old Testament is the manger in which the Christ child is laid. It is not simply the backstory; it is the story that is brought to its fullest expression and proper completion in Jesus of Nazareth. A Jesus who is divorced from the Law, the Prophets, and the Writings is not the real Jesus. He's a plastic Jesus ready to be molded to whatever agenda is at hand.

Conclusion

The kind of deliverance—that word is not too strong—needed resembles that needed by Prince Rilian at the climax of C. S. Lewis's *The Silver Chair*.[34] The fourth book[35] of the *Chronicles of Narnia*, it is the tale of Eustace Scrubb and Jill Pole's quest to find Prince Rilian, now disappeared for a decade. Joined by Puddleglum the Marshwiggle, they eventually discover Rilian in an underground pseudoworld known as Underland. Rilian is unwittingly enslaved under the enchantment of Underland's Queen, the Green Lady. The bewitched Rilian believes that Underland is the real world and that stories of Aslan and Aslan's country are just that—stories. What's worse, under the influence of the Green Lady, our heroes begin to succumb to the same illusion. Finally, at the climax, Puddleglum is shocked out of the

Green Lady's enchantments by burning his foot. In a moment of clarity, he declares:

> Suppose this black pit of a kingdom of yours is the only world. Well, it strikes me as a pretty poor one. ... We're just babies making up a game, if you're right. But four babies playing a game can make a play-world which licks your real world hollow. That's why I'm going to stand by the play-world. I'm on Aslan's side even if there isn't any Aslan to lead it, ... even if there isn't any Narnia.[36]

Puddleglum's wager seems bleak at this point in the novel. All the sensory evidence available and certainly all the political power of the rulers of Underland seem to indicate they run everything. The magic of the Green Lady is nearly irresistible. Only the pain resulting from Puddleglum's stepping in a fire breaks the illusion and leads to Rilian's rescue and the Green Lady's defeat.

I fear that much of contemporary American evangelicalism has been, like Rilian, bewitched into thinking that our current world—our current gnostic social imaginary—is in fact the real world, and accordingly our apologetic response is better directed not against those who, like the Green Lady, hold a cultural cache sufficient to define that world and to enthrall its inhabitants, but against those children and Marshwiggles—believers from the true margins—who insist that there is another, better, real world on offer. And, Marshwiggle that I am, I worry that it will take some pain to awaken us to the truth once more.

Chapter 4

ARIANISM

Imitation Salvation

The distinctiveness of the Christian identity is
bound up with the idea of "new creation," of an
event that makes a radical, decisive and unforeseen
difference in the human world: something is
brought out of nothing, life from death. Without
this conception of its foundations, the Christian
Church will inevitably "shade off" into the religious
or intellectual climate in which it finds itself ...

Rowan Williams, *Arius*

T his book is not an argument as much as an invitation to see things in a certain way: to read late modern North American evangelicalism through the lenses provided by the classical heresies. Its object is to show that the heresies illuminate something about our situation that has thus far not been considered sufficiently seriously. In one sense, then, it is an exercise in the sanctified imagination. But we are still rooted in and aiming for the truth of the thing. We want to see what is *really* there but has until now been obscured. At the halfway point, perhaps it's a good time to pause and take stock—have we described the roots well? Are we aimed at a true telos?

The roots of the exercise, I think, my critics and fellow travelers together will grant. Will anyone seriously dispute that late modern evangelicalism in North America is politicized, and polarized along culture war lines? Like G. K. Chesterton's description of sin, this is a fact "as practical as potatoes."[1] Many evangelicals have unconsciously acted to secure political position, privilege, or advantage and have done so by subsuming the gospel to one or another political agenda. This is a contemporary instantiation of Simony. The immediate consequence is to accept their preferred political agenda as the way things really are, rather than part of a good yet fallen creation needing redemption. The gospel inevitably ceases to be a call to conversion in need of occasional intellectual defense (apologetics) and becomes instead an add-on, whether idiosyncratic or essential, to an otherwise "normal life" (accommodation). If anyone needs to be converted any more, it is only those naïve, benighted believers who refuse to get with the enlightened program. This, I said, is thinly veiled gnosticism.

And now for the telos: If the description I have offered is true, what are the consequences to be expected or anticipated? I hope to answer that question in the remaining three chapters. If the gospel is part of a political program in need of implementation, then the kingdom is a project we can go a long way toward accomplishing. Pelagianism is the name for this ancient heresy in modern guise, and we'll take it up in chapter 5. If we are engaged in kingdom building, it follows that opposition to the kingdom project is not just mistaken but morally culpable. Those benighted believers need to be converted not simply because they are wrong but because they are bad people. This is a current iteration of Donatism, the topic of chapter 6.

Pelagianism and Donatism are churchly heresies. They are about the church's mission and boundaries. Before we can unpack them, we need to talk further about the church's Lord. Christian gnosticism, as we saw, was remarkably, even admirably, Christocentric. At their best, Saturninus, Valentinus, Cerinthus, and the rest sought to bring the good news of Jesus to their culture. But the culture, sadly, controlled what they believed could plausibly be said about Jesus (he was not human) and about his gospel (it was a secret message only for initiates). In this chapter, we press this contention further. If the gospel is subservient to a political message, then salvation is no longer about something God has done. It is about something we must do. And on this reading, Jesus is not the Savior but someone who teaches us to save ourselves. If we are Simoniacs and gnostics, in other words, we are invariably also Arians.

Two Cheers for Arius

I continue to try throughout this book to present the heretics, if not the heresies that have taken their names, in as sympathetic a light as possible. Simon likely was converted in some sense but, like the rootless and withered wheat (Mark 4:6), lapsed into old habits. Saturninus, Basilides, Valentinus, and Cerinthus really were Christians who valiantly tried to present Jesus to their world in a way to make him compelling—someone worth following. They were apologists and evangelists who erred by accommodating the gospel to the cultural assumptions and mores of their times and places. Pelagius and the Donatists, as we will see, were legitimately concerned about the need for holiness to mark the lives of Christian believers, especially clergy. As a result, they lost purchase on the beauty and reality of saving grace. Sympathy is a requirement of both Christian charity and simple accuracy: we stand in some sense in these heretics' debt. As Thomas Aquinas put it, "We must respect both parties, namely, those whose opinion we follow, and those whose opinion we reject. For both have diligently sought the truth and have aided us in this matter."[2]

Laudable as this may be, the task is challenging especially when introducing the fourth-century presbyter Arius, recalled in older sources as "the heresiarch"—the source of heresy. According to Rowan Williams, from the collapse of the Roman Empire until the medieval era, "Arius himself came more and more to be regarded as a kind of Antichrist among heretics, a man whose superficial austerity and spirituality cloaked a diabolical malice, a deliberate enmity to revealed faith. ... No other heretic has been through so thoroughgoing a process of 'demonization.'"[3] The reasons for this are varied and ancient, extending even to the fifth century rivalry between the Arian Goths who sacked the Empire and their Catholic civil servants who continued to administer it. Even before his death, Arius's writings were being destroyed by imperial decree, and those that survive do so only as preserved by his enemies.[4] In the Christian imagination before the late twentieth century, when it comes to Christianity's villain, only Judas the betrayer comes off worse than Arius.

The tradition is clear: Arius is the bad guy for denying the full divinity of the Son. After that, however, there seems to be little consensus about it. Perhaps Arius was a scriptural literalist who overemphasized Jesus's humanity and downplayed his divinity. Or maybe he drew on and modified Middle or Neoplatonist notions of mediation, affirming the Word as a created mediator between the transcendent Father and a wholly other creation. Yet again, maybe Arius was indebted to Jewish angelology for his understanding of mediatory creatures. Or was he really an ascetic who stressed holiness and whose savior "saved" by offering an example that disciples had to imitate? Finally, maybe Arius took the suffering of the Son in the body so seriously that he was driven to the conclusion that the Son was a creature.[5] All these hypotheses have been plausibly developed within the last two hundred years or so. All depend on the same primary sources. And while none necessarily excludes the others, they all differ.

I'm not about to offer my own new and improved interpretation of Arius.[6] Instead I want to start with an observation that is agreed upon and expand it. The scholars summarized above agree that Arius was not an innovative theologian. He did not found a school; his biblical exegesis was traditional both in method and conclusion; his doctrinal teachings were not novel. Arius did not seek self-advancement or influence like Simon Magus. He did not teach to "correct" orthodoxy like the gnostics. Rather, Arius read in the way he had been taught and taught what he had received. He did so to preserve what he understood to be the faith once given to the saints. Arius was a conservative. This observation is important because in the popular presentation of Arianism, Arius is the innovator while Athanasius is the defender of the once-for-all-faith against the world. That's romantic, surely. But it's not true.

Arius was a conservative, first of all, in his reception of the church's Trinitarian grammar. He fully affirmed the language of "Father, Son, and Holy Spirit." The language had been well entrenched in the liturgy for centuries, and Arius had no desire to change the church's manner of speech or mode of worship. Quite the opposite, in fact. He treated the language of substance (*ousia*) and person (*hypostasis*) as synonymous and asserted a real distinction (that is, a distinction of substance, *ousia*, and person, *hypostasis*) within the Trinity. In doing so, he simply carried over language of the previous generation's rejection of modal monarchianism. Found in the writings of Paul of Samosata and Sabellius, modal monarchianism stressed the absolute indivisibility of God. Accordingly, "Father, Son, and Holy Spirit" described only the modes of God's appearance in salvation history: he appeared to Israel as Father, to the disciples as Son, and to the church as Holy Spirit. Although subsequent history has concluded that Arius was a heretic, he deliberately used antiheretical language. He wanted to preserve the reality of the *trias*, the Trinity.

Arius was conservative, further, in his reading of Scripture. He insisted that his biblical exegesis merely continued that of the martyr Lucian of Antioch (which it did). Although none of Lucian's writings have survived, he is consistently reported to have taught that the Son is distinct *in being* from the Father. His relationship is not one of begetting as much as it is one of image to original. The Son is created by, distinct from, and subordinate to the Father. Here, Bible and doctrine coalesce in one of the most contentious exegetical debates in the run up to the Council of Nicaea. The debate swirled around the "beginning" of Wisdom in Proverbs 8:22–36. All sides agreed that Wisdom in this passage rightly refers to the Word, the Son, he who became incarnate as Jesus of Nazareth. Additionally, as far as Arius (and Lucianists generally) were concerned, the repeated references to the timing of Wisdom's creation meant, straightforwardly enough, that Wisdom/Logos/the Son was an exalted creature. Arius is rightly read as defending a Lucian reading and indeed natural reading of the biblical text. Preeminent in status, first in time, exalted forever—but, Arius said, there was a time when the Father was not the Father, for there was a time when the Son was not. Again, rather than daringly departing from tradition, Arius is best seen as conserving an exegetical tradition he had received.

Third, Arius was conservative in his own role in what has become known as the Nicene controversy. While it is true that Arius managed to garner popular support both within his diocese of Alexandria and outside it, and while it is true that he had numerous strong episcopal supporters among the churches of the East, he did not teach in order to cultivate such support. Rather, he seems to have been spurred to action by the teaching of his own bishop, Alexander.

To explore this last assertion properly, we need to take a little detour into Alexandrian theology. Alexandria was one of the leading centers of learning in both pagan and Christian antiquity, maintaining both Jewish and Christian exegetical schools, so it's hardly surprising that from early on it was a center of theological debate. And it's no surprise either that Origen, at least for a time, called this great city home. Origen was, like Lucian of Antioch, a biblical exegete of no small proportion. Unlike Lucian, it appears that Origen was schooled in Jewish figural interpretation of the Septuagint—effectively, his Old Testament[7]—and carried over such figural reading into his own work. Further, he was heavily indebted to the Platonic thought forms of his time, as is evidenced in his musings about the soul's relationship to the body, its preexistence, and its "fall" into materiality. In his reflections on the nature of the incarnation, Origen left an unresolved tension. He affirmed that the Son was both coeternal and subordinate to the Father. Indeed the coeternal Son was a distinct *hypostasis*, both divine and inferior to the unbegotten Father.[8] No wonder my own patristics professor, George Dragas, routinely quipped that Origen was "the father of the fathers and the father of the heretics."

Alexander became Bishop of Alexandria in 313—an auspicious time! The persecution of Emperor Diocletian had ended, and Christianity had become a tolerated religion in the empire. Bishops East and West had something they had rarely had in the first three centuries of the faith: imperially approved leisure, time for reflection and consolidation that previously had not been possible. To overcome ecclesial and doctrinal disunity occasioned by the persecution and previous leaders' responses to it, Alexander tried "to consolidate the unity of the Church around himself as Bishop by insisting upon a uniformity of teaching"[9] among all his clergy. He focused on the identity of God as Trinity, specifically on the Son's relationship to the Father. He resolved the tension in Origen in favor of coeternality. The Father and Son were united not merely in will but in substance. And it appears he expected his clergy to fall in line.

Now back to our story. In opposing his bishop, Arius once again displays his solid conservative credentials in two ways. First, to Arius's ears, Alexander seemed to obliterate any distinction of consequence between Father and Son, thus reviving the modal monarchian heresy of the previous century. And in response he does what any good conservative would—even should—do: he reiterates the teaching he received. The Son is a distinct *hypostasis* and *ousia* from the Father. He is subordinate to the Father. Where Alexander resolves Origen's tension in favor of coeternality and therefore unity-in-substance, Arius does the opposite: he maintains a distinction of substance and therefore unity in will alone. Second, Arius demonstrates his conservativism in his understanding of polity. He does not go off on his own to found another church or school (again, as both Simon and the gnostics did). Instead, he intends to remain within the church. From that position he writes to Alexander both to offer fraternal correction and to explain himself. He also writes to other bishops (notably Eusebius of Nicomedia, himself a Lucianist, who became Arius's champion at Nicaea) imploring their support. He even writes to the emperor Constantine. In none of the surviving correspondence does Arius present himself as an innovator, someone who has discovered some nugget of biblical or theological teaching previous generations had overlooked. Rather, he straightforwardly presents statements of faith that take for granted that he is merely repeating authentically catholic (that is, universal) teaching about the person of Christ. He is genuinely baffled by his persecution.

Arius receives the church's liturgy and believes he passes it on intact. He reads the Bible in the same way as the tradition in which he was raised. He at least sometimes wants to avoid schism, appealing directly to his bishop, other bishops, and even the emperor in ways that honor catholic polity and seek to preserve the unity of the church. In all of this, I like Arius. His intentions and behavior are admirable. But he's wrong. Catastrophically wrong. He deserves a sympathetic presentation. But that doesn't change what his doughty opponent, Athanasius, rightly saw: that if Arius was right, *everything* would have to change.

... but only Two

Jaroslav Pelikan helpfully summarizes Arian teaching as follows: "This Logos-Son ... was less than God but more than man, a soteriological as well as cosmological intermediary ... a Christ suspended between man and God, identical with neither but related to both."[10] In its time, this was essentially a conservative position, articulated against the heresy propounded by Paul of Samosata and Sabellius. The intention is no doubt correct: to affirm a real distinction between Father and Son. By "real," however, Arius and his supporters meant "substantive." However preeminent, the Son was a creature. As his opponents realized, this would have grave theological, soteriological, and liturgical consequences.

Theologically, Arius affirmed the transcendence of the Father. Here are Arius's own words, preserved by his opponent, Athanasius: "God himself then, as he is, is inexpressible to all. He alone has none equal or like himself."[11] Arius elaborates in this excerpt from a letter to Bishop Alexander: "We recognize one God, alone unbegotten, alone eternal, alone without beginning, alone true, alone possessing immortality, alone wise, alone good, alone Master ... unchangeable and unalterable, just and good."[12] At first blush, there is little here that is objectionable to the post-Nicene confession. Certainly orthodox Christians similarly affirm transcendence in these or very similar terms. But where we would ascribe these attributes to the blessed Trinity, Arius intends the Father only. Arius says that we adore the Father as everlasting "only through him who has come to be. The one without beginning established a Son as a beginning of things created and having engendered him bore him as his own son."[13] The implication is startling: the Father is, essentially, an unknowable mystery; as "invisible" to the Son as to the rest of creation; "inexpressible" to the Son and "unspeakable" by him.[14] The problem, as Athanasius rightly recognized, was that Christians had been preaching and worshiping for centuries as though the Son had become incarnate as Jesus of Nazareth to enable human beings not simply to know the Father but to participate in the divine nature (2 Pet 1:3–4). If Arius's unnuanced affirmation of transcendence is right, then traditional Christian assertions about the knowability of the Father through the incarnation of the Son are wrong.

Soteriologically, the question is even more fraught. Arius feared that Alexander was reintroducing the old Sabellian heresy, in which the only distinction between Father and Son is timing and mode of revelation. If this is the case, however, then the Logos shares fully in the divine attributes of simplicity and impassibility.[15] Arius appears to have reasoned further (or at least some of those sympathetic to his position did[16]) that if the Son is impassible, he did not suffer. But the Scriptures insist that he did. If the Son *really* suffered, he cannot be coeternal with the Father.[17] How then is the suffering of the Son said to be saving in Arius's model? In this way: because the Son is a creature (even the *preeminent* creature) his divine status is not essential but attained through his free and entire union of his will to God's. The entirety of this unity of will is displayed in the incarnation and fully and finally in the suffering that culminated in the cross. All this the Son accomplishes for himself, providing an example for human disciples to imitate. If we lesser creatures would attain adoption by the divine, we must imitate Christ and unite ourselves to God even unto death, as Christ himself did. The problem (again called out by Athanasius) is that the Scriptures and the liturgy together affirm that Christ is the Savior, not that we save ourselves by following Christ's example and certainly not that he himself needs saving. If Arius's soteriology is right, then the Son is not the Savior.

Finally, in the Arian debate, theology and soteriology coalesced—as they always do—in public Christian worship. Here especially, Arius's own conservative tendencies undid his position. He wanted nothing to change, but as we've seen, if he was right, everything had to, including the way Christians prayed.

> Whether angel or Son of God, the Arian Logos, though subordinate to the Father and not of the same *ousia* as him, was nevertheless worthy of worship. The Arians shared with other Christians the usage of praying to the Son of God an adoration that by right belonged to God alone. ... The Arians found prayer to the Logos an unavoidable element of Christian worship.[18]

And in this, as their critics from Athanasius to Gregory of Nazianzus to Ambrose never tired of pointing out, the Arians were defeated by their own inconsistency. It does look as though, following Origen and some forms of Jewish mysticism, groups of Arian Christians tried to temper their prayers to the Logos,[19] but they all (rightly) refused to tinker with the baptismal formula. Arian Christians were baptized into the name of the Father, the Son, and the Holy Spirit. But by their own definitions, this would either idolatrously raise two creatures to the rank of Father, or it would recognize the divine status of three beings, reintroducing polytheism. If the prayers and rites of the faithful implicitly recognized the divinity of the Son (and the Holy Spirit), then Arius was wrong. If Arius was right, over three centuries of Christian worship would have to be retooled.

It is thus one of the ironies of Christian history that an inherently conservative theological teacher, defending a traditional hermeneutic and Christology, was finally defeated (almost fifty years after his death) by a radical innovation—a new theological word, and an extrabiblical one at that, that went to the root of our understanding of the Son's relationship to the Father. That word was *homoousios*, meaning "of the same substance." Its inclusion in the creeds of Nicaea and Constantinople cemented what we now take for granted to be essential, biblical truths: (1) The Word *is* the utterance of the Father from all eternity (that is, the Son reveals the Father simply by *being* the Son). (2) The Son suffers not just alongside us, but as one of us, for us, representing us, and indeed in place of us. In so doing, he saves us. (3) Christians worship the Son and the Holy Spirit as God because Son and Spirit are of the *ousia* of the Father: with the Father they comprise the Godhead.

Here we shall always be indebted to Arius for forcing what became orthodoxy to distinguish between *ousia* (substance) and *hypostasis* (person) in a way that hadn't been done before and to justify its conclusions biblically rather than merely speculatively. These necessary intricacies aside, however, the basic argument is simple: Christians worship God alone; Christians worship the Son as God; therefore, the Son is God. Two cheers, but only two, for Arius.

Evangelical Arians?

Evangelicals are a pragmatic bunch. It's the product of our DNA. If we are a renewal movement within Protestant Christianity whose helix interweaves biblicism, crucicentrism, conversionism, and activism, it follows inevitably that we will likely embrace anything that enables us to take the biblical message of the cross to those who have yet to be converted by it. Examples from our history abound. Christians have been worshiping in the evening or night as long as there have been Christians. But gearing the evening service explicitly to evangelism seems to be a uniquely evangelistic response to "facts on the ground" in the early twentieth century. Aimee Semple McPherson, for instance, embraced newly developed electrical lights as she "hollywoodized" her revival meetings with sets and lights to heighten the visual presentation of herself and her message.[20] She was hardly alone in her embrace of technology. Even stereotypically staid Canadians adopted similar strategies to win the lost.[21] Crusade-style preaching, often associated with Billy Graham, grew out of the Great Awakening and the commitment of John Wesley in England and George Whitefield in the United States to bring the gospel to where the people were, rather than waiting for them to come to church. In Wesley's case, ironically, the action was at first forced by Anglican bishops who literally locked their church doors to his ministry. Today, Roman Catholic forays into mass media communication, from Archbishop Fulton Sheen to Bishop Robert Barron, take paths well worn by previous generations of evangelicals and charismatics. When it comes to the faith, we are a practical people.

This commitment to pragmatism also infects our approach to theology. Evangelicals have not been known for their influence in the guild of systematic or academic theologians, or at least not until recently.[22] Our theology seldom rises to that level of abstraction: it's far more often focused on popularizing the good theology of others. Those evangelical theologians who have most influenced my own life and work, J. I. Packer, John Stott, and Michael Green, are excellent thinkers who strive to be unoriginal and want instead to communicate the wisdom of earlier ages to modern readers in an accessible way. They are pastoral theologians, whose work is aimed at the formation of preachers and laypeople for the sake of evangelism and activism. This commitment to making theology accessible is a strength. The flip side, however, is a glaring weakness: it can lead to a tendency to dismiss academic theology entirely. "Who cares whether it's useful as long as it's true?" is not a rhetorical question evangelicals pose of doctrines. It's more like this: "If it's not useful, it's not important. And if it's not important, it can be ignored." I run into this objection regularly in my own work in the formation of pastors—and at one level I get it. Academic theology does deal in abstraction. The subject matter is hard. Its applicability to the life of the average pastor or layperson is not often immediately apparent. And frankly, academic theologians across the board don't make it easier by not knowing how to write. Still, I try to convince my students that while not all doctors should strive to be neurosurgeons, general practitioners who sneer at the specialists are not good doctors. So it is for physicians of the soul. Even if we are not called to ivory-tower levels of abstraction, we should thank God that some are and that others see the need to make that work accessible to us for the sake of our ministries.

Even in our Christology—our study of the person and work of Jesus—evangelicals tend to put the doctrine's usefulness ahead of its truth. Perhaps no other group of Protestants has so fully taken to heart Philip Melanchthon's objection to the Christology of the "school men":

> We do better to adore the mysteries of deity than to investigate them. What is more, these matters cannot be probed without great danger, and even holy men have often experienced this. ... Therefore, there is no reason why we should labour so much on those exalted topics, such as "God," "the unity and trinity of God," "the mystery of creation" and "the manner of the incarnation." What, I ask you, did the scholastics accomplish during the many ages they were examining only these points? ... But as for one who is ignorant of the fundamentals— namely "the power of sin," "the law" and "grace"—I do not see how I can call him a Christian. For from these things Christ is known, since to know Christ means to know his benefits and not, as they [the scholastics] teach, to reflect upon his natures and the modes of his incarnation. For unless you know why Christ put on flesh and was nailed to the cross, what good will it do you to know merely the history about him? ... Christ was given us as a remedy and, to use the language of Scripture, a saving remedy. It

is therefore proper that we know Christ in another way than that which the scholastics have set forth.[23]

We do not deny the incarnation. Indeed, we continue to affirm Nicaea and Chalcedon.[24] In *The Cross of Christ*, John Stott has no interest in novelty or pressing his own research agenda. He offers instead a thoroughly traditional, unoriginal presentation of the major biblical and theological threads that, woven together, produce the doctrine of the work of Christ. The most that can be said about Stott's agenda is that he is particularly concerned to articulate a modest understanding of penal substitution aimed at blunting the objections and excesses of critics and defenders alike who misunderstand and misconstrue it.[25] But this is only one part of the book, which as a whole is about resourcing preachers and laity alike to contemplate, proclaim, and so be formed by, the wisdom and power of God (1 Cor 1:24).

It is not controversial then to say that evangelical Christology skews toward function. And this brings us round again to Arianism. I begin with the semi-Arian Christology of Friedrich Schleiermacher. Schleiermacher, the founder of German Liberal Protestantism, was raised a Moravian and a Pietist—a "pre-evangelical," if you like. Today he would have had Wesleyan/Holiness roots much like mine. Schleiermacher claimed both to preserve and to move beyond his Pietist identity when he described himself as a "Moravian of a higher order" later in life. He discerned a deep connection between the spirituality in which he was raised and the liberal theology he founded. This was not accidental and was thus a good warning to those evangelicals who are both

Pietists and their heirs. We are not as removed from Arianism as we like to think.

But back to Schleiermacher. As we saw in chapter 2, he was a brilliant apologist, hoping to make Christian faith accessible and attractive to a new generation of Romantics, the cultured despisers of both the Enlightenment project and the confessional rationalist theology that it produced. This spirited defense of the faith continued in his magnum opus, *The Christian Faith*.[26] There he argued that Christian doctrine was not about truth or ethics but about *feeling*—the German word is *Gefühl*.[27] By this he meant not mere emotion but the basic orientation of human beings toward God: absolute dependence, or God-consciousness. Schleiermacher would take the entire body of Christian doctrine and reread it according to such *feeling*. How do Christian doctrines preserve, elicit, or strengthen the feeling of absolute dependence, or God-consciousness? That is the question that drives Schleiermacher's dogmatic exposition.

What is the result of this move with respect to the doctrine of the person of Christ? For Schleiermacher, Christ alone among humanity has a fully developed God-consciousness. So deep and developed was that awareness in Christ's person that he may be recognized as the incarnation of God and uniquely spoken of as God's Son. The record of Christ's God-consciousness is found in the Scriptures, especially the Gospels. To access the Redeemer— Schleiermacher's favorite title for the Lord—is to search for him there. The feeling of absolute dependence further frees us with respect to the Bible in the following way: those parts of the Bible that do not enlighten us with respect to the Redeemer or elicit within us a similar feeling of God-consciousness may safely be set aside. Thus believers are freed from the embarrassing bits, whether the morally reprehensible stories of the Old Testament or the unbelievable miracle stories of the New. We need neither defend nor debunk them; we simply set them aside as irrelevant. Doctrinally, we are freed from the overly Platonic, unbiblical accretions inherited in the Nicene and Chalcedonian formulations. It's not so much that they are false (though they quite likely are) as that they are irrelevant to the description of Christ's God-consciousness.

With respect to Christ's work, the doctrine of redemption, we end in a similar place. Redemption for Schleiermacher results from the meditation of believers on the life of the Redeemer, especially his passion, which thereby elicits, raises, and perfects God-consciousness in them. It is, in other words, a form of exemplarism in which believers save themselves by meditating on the example of Jesus. We find the life of the Redeemer in the Bible, in the community of disciples who share in that life, and in the means of grace by which we enter and are continually strengthened in that community. The evidence of redemption, finally, is simply living out our own God-consciousness in imitation of Christ's. The indispensability of Scripture, church, sacrament, and sanctification are affirmed. Once again, however, those passages of Scripture that trouble us, whether the blood-drenched altars of Leviticus, or the picayune dietary requirements of

Deuteronomy, or the blood-soaked battlefields of Joshua, can be easily ignored, as can an unhealthy preoccupation with the traditional doctrinal language of atonement (and of penal substitution in particular).

I have traveled quickly (but I hope fairly) over Schleiermacher's Christology. Before I tease out some contemporary similarities, let me offer an assessment. First, it is right to describe it as an early example of a functional Christology. The identity of Jesus Christ is discerned in his experience of a complete God-consciousness, a psychological category and activity. His saving work is found in the awakening of God-consciousness in the lives of believers. To move from there to label Schleiermacher an Arian, however, is unfair. As we've seen, he affirms the incarnation, sort of. And from there, he goes on to defend the doctrine of the Trinity, even if he doesn't quite know what to do with it, relegating it to the concluding chapter of *The Christian Faith*. By attenuating the biblical witness and dismissing centuries of doctrinal development, stressing the function of the Redeemer over the substance of his person as the essence of incarnation, Schleiermacher opens a door that later generations of liberal Protestant preachers were not afraid to walk through. The Redeemer was a creature—an exalted, distinct, entirely God-conscious creature. Similarly, it is hard to see how Schleiermacher's doctrine of atonement evades the charge of exemplarism. The fact that "Redeemer" was Schleiermacher's favorite sobriquet for Christ is a red herring. The Bible (or portions of it), church, and sacrament may well be necessary, but in the end we save ourselves by meditating on the God-consciousness of the Redeemer and letting it well up within us. We sanctify ourselves by following him in so uniting our will to God's that we will not shy away from suffering even unto death, just as Christ embraced the cross. The charge of semi-Arianism is, it seems to me, justifiable.

The journey of liberal Protestantism from Melanchthon's move away from ontology to the benefits of Christ, through Schleiermacher's doctrine of God-consciousness, through the various Arianisms of twentieth-century liberal Protestantism, to the most cursory glances at the emptiness, silliness, and straight up Unitarian Protestant and evangelical Protestant contemporary worship, all points to a truth that ought to unsettle every Protestant. The loss of theological purchase on Christ's person and work culminates in Arianism of some sort. As a result, *everything* sooner or later changes, and never for the better. Liberal Protestantism has lost Jesus, and in so doing has lost its soul. Are we evangelicals that far behind? I worry that we are not.

An Arian Christology is preaching and spiritual formation that puts Jesus to work serving this or that political issue, which is believed for other, more important reasons. The Arian Jesus is a cheerleader for securing the border or opening it, for constraining abortion access or widening it, for banning guns or buying them. Pick a hot-button political issue, and you will find someone insisting Jesus is exclusively on their side. But Jesus is not a creature; he is not of this world. His gospel is not a message about how to build a kingdom. His gospel is that in his vicarious life, death, and resurrection, he—the God-man—has delivered us from the unholy reign of sin, death, and the devil. Oh, he is a king, and his kingdom is breaking in all around us. But it's his kingdom, not ours. It is not of this world. Unsurprisingly, this is merely a reiteration of the charge made with respect to the Bible in chapter 2. Like the Scriptures that testify to him, the Arian Jesus is a wax nose twisted this way and that to support political positions that he never addressed in the Gospels and of which the Scriptures that testify to him know nothing directly. He is a "a noneschatological, present-tense, this-world-affirming Jesus" who's entirely beholden to opposed ideologies.[28] Whether right or left, traditional or radical, the Arian Jesus of politically compromised evangelicalism falls to the same criticism George Tyrrell famously laid at the feet of Adolf von Harnack: "The Christ that Harnack sees, looking back through nineteen centuries of Catholic darkness, is only the reflection of a liberal Protestant face, seen at the bottom of a deep well."[29]

Arianism's Solution: Incarnation

If the solution to Simony is prudence, and gnosticism is cured by realism, then the forsaking of Arianism is an embrace of a full-blooded doctrine of the incarnation. One that *does* care about natures and attributes and the preoccupations of the schoolmen, since it cares about the identity of the person of the Redeemer. Furthermore, while I'm sure our seminary classrooms would benefit from students (and professors) being formed in the Nicene faith in and through their theology classes, I have something far more practical in mind: Christian worship. If Arius taught his heretical Christology in part through hymns, and Athanasius insisted that centuries of orthodox worship had implicitly affirmed the *homoousios*, that is where we ought to focus our attention too. I offer three suggestions, in ascending order of controversy.

First, evangelicals could begin the arduous road of repenting of and learning to "unthink" their Arianism by confessing the Nicene Creed in worship. Before it is a doctrinal standard, a summation and snapshot of history, or some sort of ordination gatekeeper, a creed is the intellectual expression of faith. It is an act of worship. "God of God, Light of Light begotten. Behold, he abhors not the Virgin's womb! Very God, begotten not created. O come let us adore him." Singing the second stanza of "O Come All Ye Faithful" two or three times per year is probably as close as most North American evangelicals come to confessing Nicaea.[30] That's not good enough. In its proper context, the creed is part of the response of our entire selves to the good news of God in the gospel. We hear from God in his Word, announced in Scripture and sermon. We then respond to God with the creed (our mental assent), the prayers (our intentional assent), and the offering (our substantial assent). Finally the climax: we offer ourselves, our souls and bodies, by receiving God's incarnate life in Holy Communion. Without the creed, our response is lacking, for there is no form through which to express mental assent.

Second, evangelicals could continue by reading *with* Nicaea—in other words, by allowing the creed to control our understanding of Scripture. This is *not* the insertion of a foreign standard to constrain the word of God. Far from it. It is the Spirit-guided summary of the Scriptures in the mind of the whole church that leads us into the right reading of the word of God (1 Cor 2:16). For New Testament scholars this might mean translating with Nicaea in mind.

That Nicea disclosed the inner logic of Scripture was settled in 381 when the Nicene Creed was ratified and expanded by Constantinople. Those evangelicals who continue to insist on "no creed but the Bible!" do not actually free themselves from creedal interference. They merely set themselves up as the hermeneutical standard by which they will determine what the Scriptures mean. If we confess Nicaea in our worship, however, the right of private interpretation is no longer ours. We read in accord with and in submission to the church catholic—that is, Roman, Orthodox, and classical Protestants—and not on our own. We read with Nicaea and thereby find in the Scriptures he who is the only begotten of the Father, God the only begotten God (John 1:18).

Allow me, finally, to broaden that last paragraph, which I expect rankled at least the "soul liberty"–affirming Baptists among my readers. Evangelicals can repent of their Arianism by rightly blessing Mary as *theotokos*, the Mother of God, in both corporate and private prayer. The term *theotokos* comes up in church history a century after Nicaea, with the eruption of the Nestorian controversy and the Council of Ephesus (431), which enshrined the first Marian title—*theotokos*, bearer or Mother of

God—as dogma to preserve the unity of the person of Christ. Mary gave birth, Ephesus concluded, not to a human nature to which a divine nature was affixed, but to a person who was and forever remains the human instantiation of the Second Person of the blessed Trinity, the man who is God. But precisely as such, Mary rightly guards against a revival of Arianism. The person of Christ is not "divine" with scare quotes affixed, an exalted creature. He is God, being of one substance with the Father. Furthermore, inviting evangelicals to thank God regularly for she who said yes to the greatest invitation of all time—to bear the Word in heart and body—is not to promote those aspects of Catholic piety that are completely foreign to evangelical conviction and experience. It is simply to conform to the Mother of God's own observation in Luke 1:48–49: "For behold, from now on all generations will call me blessed; for he who is mighty has done great things for me, and holy is his name." Let us take our place among the generations who call her blessed!

Incorporating reflection on the person of Christ more explicitly into our public and private piety will free us from politicizing Jesus because it will remind us that he comes *from the outside*. He is not a creature, however exalted, who comes with a message of self-salvation. He is not a king with a this-worldly cause, however noble. Otherwise his followers would fight for him (John 18:36).[31] He and his kingdom are not of this world. His gospel is that he has come to destroy the works of the devil, to end the ancient serpent's reign, and to sit on his father David's throne forever. In his incarnate life, from conception to ascension and beyond, this is exactly what has happened. And precisely for that reason he will never be the champion of any political program other than his own. He pulls down the mighty from their seats, and the rich he sends away empty. He calls us to follow him, and blesses no ideology we have made.

Conclusion

It has been said that John Henry Newman's nineteenth-century writings on Arius and Arianism tell the careful reader much more about their author than about their subject.[32] Whether deliberately, accidentally, or even despite authorial intent, books disclose much about their authors. This is especially true of Newman's *Arians of the Fourth Century* (1833). When it was first published, in addition to being a scholarly study of an ancient heresy, it not-so-subtly defended Newman's rejection of the heavily evangelical piety of the Victorian Church of England into which he had been converted. Furthermore, it justified Newman's founding—along with Pusey, Keble, and others—of the Oxford Movement, with its attempt to reclaim the Church of England's pre-Reformation heritage. Three decades later, after his reception into the Roman Catholic Church, Newman would recast *Arians of the Fourth Century* in a different light in his *Apologia Pro Vita Sua*. Though the Newman of *Arians* did not grasp it at the time, the Newman of the *Apologia* saw it as the moment when he concluded that the Church of England—low-church evangelical, latitudinarian, and Anglo-Catholic all fractiously fitted together—was a doomed project. It was Arianism or Rome. Newman opted for the latter.

The gravity of Newman's conclusion cannot be underestimated. As he recalled his life in the *Apologia*, Newman understood that his time in the Oxford Movement was about slowly confronting and accepting the impossible: the Church of England neither would nor could recover its catholic heritage, and even the attempt to do so only produced a "catholic" church that adopted some practices but left others behind based at best on aesthetics. What remained, however improbable, was, for Newman, the truth. The extreme party—Roman Catholicism—was all that was left. In 1841 Newman became the most famous Roman Catholic convert in the English-speaking world. The Catholic community in England was, at the time, socially marginal and legally suspect. Even worse, it was the religion of the Irish. Where today we often change churches like we change our shoes, this move cost Newman greatly: he forsook security, respect, and position for a communion where he was never truly welcome (even if today he is a Roman Catholic saint). But in a sense the choice had been made for him, simply because he believed he had come to the truth.

The point is not that readers ought to become Roman Catholic. Rather, like Newman, we are on the threshold of a choice with grave consequences. If we subsume the gospel to politics and make the good news of salvation a mere addendum, we will lose Jesus as surely as Arius did. Arius—biblical scholar, theological conservative, philosophically conversant—thought he was resolving a problem bequeathed to his generation by Origen. Had it succeeded, his argument that the Son was an exalted creature begotten in time would have put to rest forever the bugaboo of modal monarchianism. It preserved the transcendence and preeminence of the Father and freed the church from misattributing suffering to the divine. The subordination of the Son to the Father, further, seemed to have solid the Scriptural support of both Testaments.

Where he finally failed, however, was in his insistence that the piety of the church would not change. He insisted that prayers would still be offered to Jesus after a fashion; that the baptismal formula needed no alteration; that Jesus was still the Savior. Though he lacked Arius's subtlety, Athanasius could see what Arius could not: if the Son was a creature, everything had to change. If the Son was subordinate to the Father in being, the worship properly afforded the Son of God had to be reduced to mere veneration, akin to that afforded to Mary and the saints by the Roman Catholic Church. For like them, he was a creature. And what's worse, if he was a creature, then he was not the Savior. The ascetic message of unity-in-suffering he brought was not itself salvation but the means by which humans would save themselves.

Is that the Jesus we wish to embrace? For that is what the political Jesus on offer today can give us. He does not give us himself in the Spirit, through word and sacrament. He does not by his very life unite us to the life of God. He gives us a program which, if we implement it, will save us and even the world. It may sound good, but it's not the gospel. That Jesus is not the Lord. And in the next two chapters, I'll invite you to see why.

Chapter 5

PELAGIANISM

We Will Build the Kingdom

———————

For the man of today hope no longer means looking for things over which we have no control, but action by our own power. Man expects redemption to come from himself and he seems to be in a position to provide it.

Pope Benedict XVI, *Faith and the Future*

L arge swaths of North American evangelicalism, especially among its elite, have subordinated the gospel to politics in order to maintain cultural cachet and influence. Not limited to the right or left, the sellout has a hold on all sides. Indeed that very division, so easily assumed, is indicative of the depth of the problem. I called this Simony and suggested two inevitable entanglements. (1) The transformation of the gospel from an announcement of an event (this Jesus whom you crucified has been raised from the dead) to a disembodied message of personal and/or social transformation—a political program. In short, gnosticism. (2) The reduction of the gospel from the mighty act of God interrupting the downward spiral of human damnation by the taking up of human nature to a message of self and social sanctification in imitation of Christ—that is, Arianism. The focus of chapters 3 and 4 has thus been doctrinal: our embrace of the primacy of politics leads invariably to a loss of not only of the humanity and deity of Christ and the unity of his person but also the glorious gospel announcement that human nature has been redeemed by the incarnation, life, death, resurrection, and ascension of the God-man. In its place, we have been fed a thin gruel of moral training from the right and social justice from the left.

That saltless alternative is the focus of the next two chapters. We move from my perception that the gospel is being replaced by something that looks an awful lot like doctrinal dead-ends the church has already taken in the past, to sketch the practical consequences of the pursuit. We move, in other words, from heretical teaching to heretical practice. Once the gospel becomes a political program, once it is no longer an announcement about the act of God, we become the agents responsible for the accomplishment of that program. This is the revivification of Pelagianism. Once Pelagianism is embraced, it is a very short step to buying into the worst behavior of the hyperpartisan wider culture: the demonization of dissent. People who will not get with the program are not simply wrong, but evil. I shall explore this contention by turning to Donatism in chapter 6.

Let's begin by going back to the British monk, moralist, and foil for Augustine of Hippo, Pelagius. He was not as fantastic as the wonderworker Simon Magus nor as learned as the gnostics of earlier centuries nor as credentialed as Arius (he wasn't even ordained). Pelagius is perhaps the most genuinely humble and holy of all the heretics we have or will talk about in this book. He was a fifth-century British monk whose preaching, spiritual direction, and lifestyle had a profound impact wherever he found himself—Britain, Rome, North Africa, or Palestine. He was animated by a concern for holiness lived out among believers and put his teaching faithfully into personal practice. I remember well when I first encountered Pelagius in a church history class in college. After his views on freedom and responsibility, sin and grace were summarized by my professor, I leaned over to my friend beside me and asked, "What's wrong with that?"

What's wrong with that, indeed! We'll get to what's wrong in later sections. First we have to talk about what Pelagius got so very right.

Pelagius Redeemed (Mostly)

To do so, we need to begin with a quick look at the world in which Pelagius lived—and not only Pelagius but every Christian before him. The Greco-Roman world into which the gospel came was one in which the Fates ruled. The classical era was almost entirely fatalistic—men and women and even the gods were ruled by fate. Homer's poems and Plato's philosophy did accentuate human responsibility, skill, and even luck—virtue was impossible without these. But in the end, Homer's Olympian gods bowed to doom, and Plato's "God could not oppose destiny."[1] Socratic self-mastery, it seems, was the exception that proved the rule. If classical antiquity railed against fate but could not escape it, later Greco-Roman Hellenism seemed quite comfortable with it. In philosophy, Stoics like Cicero encouraged equanimity in the face of all circumstances, because all events were foreordained. Among the masses, divine will was replaced by astrology. Your fate and mine were unalterably written in the stars. Everyone, it seemed, had a role. If we had any contribution to make, it was only how that would be played out: nobly or not. Human life was, as a result, tragic: neither pessimistic nor nihilistic, it was an attempt to find joy and meaning in the face of an unescapable end.[2]

Into this deterministic world came early Christian preachers and thinkers with a startling anthropological shift in thinking: human beings were free and responsible before a God who called them into covenant with him. The early Christians did not invent this, of course; they inherited it from the Jews and the first Jewish followers of Jesus. Fate was replaced by divine care for creation: providence supplanted tragedy. The tragic search for meaning in the face of inevitability was replaced by a covenantal relationship with God that God himself had initiated and perfected through the incarnation, death, and resurrection of Jesus. Whether we examine the apologists like Justin Martyr or Clement of Alexandria, early theologians like Irenaeus, Tertullian, or Origen, or even later theologians including Pelagius's archfoe, Augustine, providence did not annihilate human freedom but grounded it. While the exact relationship between the two might not have been explicitly worked out, the early Christians insisted that they did not conflict. See, for example, Origen's writing on prayer:

> Through prayer, he shall come to share in the Word of God who stands in the midst even of those who do not know him, who disregards the prayer of nobody, and who prays to the Father together with the one on whose behalf he mediates. For the Son of God is high priest of our offerings and advocate with the Father (1 Jn 2:1). He prays on behalf of those who pray and acts as advocate together with those who plead.[3]

Compare that with Augustine on divine foreknowledge, human freedom, and astrology:

> We assert both that God knows all things before they come to pass, and that we do by our free will whatsoever we know and feel to be done by us only because we will it. But that all things come to pass by fate, we do not say; nay we affirm that nothing comes to pass by fate; for we demonstrate that the name of fate, as it is wont to be used by those who speak of fate, meaning thereby the position of the stars at the time of each one's conception or birth, is an unmeaning word, for astrology itself is a delusion.[4]

In the early church, in fact, the ones who understood the human propensity to sin in terms of inevitability were the gnostics (whom we've already met).[5] They were thinking too much like the Greeks they were and not enough like the Jewish believers who gave them the gospel. When writing against the gnostics, the fathers with one voice affirmed that God held human beings responsible for their behavior, called them to obey his commands, and endued them with power to obey or not. Thus they preserved "both the Christian doctrine of the goodness of the Creator and the Christian doctrine of the responsibility of the creature in opposition to a theology that denied them both by subjecting God and man to the slavery of an all-powerful fate."[6]

Pelagius's message, then, was not unprecedented. When he moved from Britain to Rome, he was confronted by what he regarded as the worldliness of the urbane Roman Christians.

Coming from a monastic environment on the fringes of the empire, he was naturally taken aback. This did not, however, make him reconsider the twin pillars of freedom and responsibility upon which his message of holy living rested. Rather, it seems to have intensified his message. Pelagius appears to have taught that God would not command what we could not obey. In this he was squarely in line with centuries of Christian moral theology. Furthermore, while it is often quipped that he denied both human sinfulness and the need for grace, this was not quite true. In Pelagius's thinking, it was God's grace that had created humans with the freedom to sin or not in the first place. Adam's sin is his alone, but its record is graciously passed on to us as a bad example. Salvation was graciously available to all who would take up their cross and follow. God graciously forgave the past sins (by faith alone!) of all who repented. God provided many gracious aids along the way to help the faithful withstand current temptations. Human freedom itself, the rational capacity to discern the good, and the volitional power to pursue it as the free creations of God—these are nothing other than grace at work. Moreover, God has disclosed his will and commands in Holy Scripture, and God has graciously given to us the example of Jesus Christ, the Word made flesh. Put charitably, if Pelagius did not collapse the distinction between grace and nature outright, he minimized it to a hair's breadth. For Pelagius, grace accompanies all people, helping them do what is in their natural power to do: seek forgiveness for past sins, avoid sin, pursue virtue in the present, and attain the holiness without which no one shall see God in the future.

One popular (but very helpful) account of the Pelagian controversy summarized the teaching like this: "Ungrateful creatures ... go on whining about our weaknesses and begging for more grace when what we really needed was to jolly well get on with our part in salvation—doing the right thing!"[7] This summary makes Pelagius sound like an early version of Jordan Peterson: "Clean your room!"[8] And the comparison is apt. Peterson himself, though grumpy, is a strong advocate for individual moral renewal that takes the capacity for such renewal for granted (even if it needs outside support from time to time—though I'm not sure he would call that grace). Not unlike Pelagius, who gathered a coterie of disciples around him who implemented his unsparing message, many people (especially young men) have found hope in Peterson's clarion call to personal responsibility.

Of course it makes sense that a spiritual director confronted with worldliness should become exasperated with people. But that exasperation was not foundational. Pelagius could exhort his wealthy patrons to lives of strict moral and spiritual discipline *optimistic* about human nature. Given the right formation and education, cooperating with all God's gifts of grace so liberally distributed through our natural abilities, the church, and the whole of creation, we could become saints.

In 410, the Visigoths sacked Rome, and Pelagius fled with his wealthy patrons first to North Africa and eventually to

Palestine. A cinematic account of his flight would have had him pass through Hippo Regius or perhaps Carthage and debate his great nemesis, Augustine, directly. But that did not happen. Though there is a tantalizing but slim record of correspondence,[9] the two never met. The journey through North Africa neverthe-less did introduce Augustine and Pelagius to each other's ideas, and though the surviving correspondence is scant, it is surpris-ingly warm. At first blush, that warmth makes sense—Pelagius, a monk and spiritual director driven by a vision of holiness for the laity, would have much to talk about with Augustine, who himself founded a monastic order and whose surviving letters and sermons demonstrate no less a concern than Pelagius for holy living. It did not take long, however, for Augustine to turn his considerable rhetorical and episcopal power against the British monk's ideas, especially as these were expressed by Pelagius's fol-lowers, Celestius and Julian of Eclanum.

Augustine's Realism

The painful points of disagreement between Augustine and Pelagius had nothing to do with the identity of God as Trinity or the Son as consubstantial with the Father. This has led some scholars to question whether Pelagius rightly wears the scarlet *H* (a question that has my sympathy, if not my support). Further, the disagreement was not over the need for holiness among God's people. Both set the bar high for those in their care. Both empha-sized the imitation of Christ's own example. And both—albeit in different ways—stressed the importance of God's cooperative grace as believers grew in sanctity. When we get to grace, however, we are moving toward the points of rupture between the two fifth-century leaders.

First, if both agreed that God's grace is real, they defined it very differently. For Pelagius, grace was not just an addition to nature (which Augustine would have also affirmed), grace was continuous with nature. God had given human beings gifts from their birth, which, if they got on with the job, were all they needed to get to heaven. (There is an open question here whether this way of understanding grace was actually Pelagius's own. As a spiritual director, he seems to have been far more interested in practice than theory. The Pelagianism against which Augustine inveighed was more likely formulated by Julian of Eclanum—but that need not detain us.[10]) For Augustine, on the other hand, while grace was a gift added to nature, it was much more than that: it was a divine interruption in and overturning of—a true revolution in—the life of sin. Believers after baptism did indeed need to cooperate with grace to grow in sanctity, but what moved them from unfaith to faith and from unbelief to belief in the first place? For Pelagius, it was the unencumbered rationality of human beings to discern the good, and the free will of human beings to choose it, that initiated the process. For Augustine, it was only the gracious intervention of God that could free the sin-bound will to do what it otherwise could not: flee to Christ and be saved. The question then is similar to one that lay between

Arius and Athanasius in the previous chapter: does grace help us save ourselves, or does grace save us?

There was no greater example of the latter understanding than Augustine himself, whose *Confessions* narrated his own dramatic conversion experience. The climax of this testimony is Book VIII of the *Confessions*. It opens with Augustine's lament that, having forsaken his life of sin, having joined with his friends on a search for God, and having come to the intellectual conclusion that Christianity is true, he nevertheless remained powerless to convert himself. His convictions certain, he still cannot make himself a Christian. In the mystery of iniquity, he concludes, the mind cannot command the mind:

> Whence is this monstrousness? and to what end? Let Thy mercy gleam that I may ask, if so be the secret penalties of men, and those darkest pangs of the sons of Adam, may perhaps answer me.
>
> Whence is this monstrousness? and to what end? The mind commands the body, and it obeys instantly; the mind commands itself, and is resisted. The mind commands the hand to be moved; and such readiness is there, that command is scarce distinct from obedience. Yet the mind is mind, the hand is body. The mind commands the mind, its own self, to will, and yet it doth not.
>
> Whence this monstrousness? and to what end? It commands itself, I say, to will, and would not command, unless it willed, and what it commands is not done. But

it willeth not entirely: therefore doth it not command entirely. For so far forth it commandeth, as it willeth: and, so far forth is the thing commanded, not done, as it willeth not. For the will commandeth that there be a will; not another, but itself. But it doth not command entirely, therefore what it commandeth, is not. For were the will entire, it would not even command it to be, because it would already be.

It is therefore no monstrousness partly to will, partly to will, but a disease of the mind, that it doth not wholly rise, by truth upborne, borne down by custom. And therefore are there two wills, for that one of them is not entire: and what the one lacketh, the other hath.[11]

We shall revisit "the darkest pangs of the sons of Adam" below. For now we note only that Augustine's condition is such that if his faith depends on him, his end is doomed: in his own words, he "all but did it, but did it not."[12] Only God could convert him, and God, it seems, was in no hurry to remedy Augustine's anguished soul: "Thou, O Lord, how long? how long, Lord, wilt Thou be angry for ever? Remember not our former iniquities, for I felt that I was held by them. I sent up these sorrowful words: How long, how long, 'to-morrow, and tomorrow?' Why not now? why not is there this hour an end to my uncleanness?"[13]

It was an overwhelming, apparently irresistible grace that finally moved the great saint's soul to faith. Sitting in his friend

Alypius's garden, hearing a child next door singing, "Take and read, take and read," he returned to Paul's Epistle to the Romans, where he read perhaps the strangest conversion text ever: "Let us walk properly as in the daytime, not in orgies and drunkenness, not in sexual immorality and sensuality, not in quarreling and jealousy. But put on the Lord Jesus Christ, and make no provision for the flesh, to gratify its desires" (Rom 13:13–14). Augustine had, by this time, put off the flesh. And now, at last, God in his grace met him: "No further would I read; nor needed I: for instantly at the end of this sentence, by a light as it were of serenity infused into my heart, all the darkness of doubt vanished away."[14]

Is grace our own natural ability along with several additions, or is it a disruptive, divinely initiated encounter that raises, heals, and empowers the will? Beneath these two ultimately opposed understandings of grace lay two similarly opposed understandings of sin. For Pelagius, grace indeed accompanied both the will to do the good and the act itself, but grace was itself dependent on the free decision of the human will.[15] Sin, in this view, was the product of accumulated sins. Adam's disobedience to the divine command was Adam's alone. The sin was his alone, as was the guilt. What was passed on to his progeny was an *example* of sinning that was all-too-easily imitated by his descendants. Original sin, we might say, is the acquired habit of sinning into which we are born. So, yes, "all have sinned" as the apostle says (Rom 3:23), but not because it is our condition to do so. Rather, the condition of sinning results from being surrounded by sinners. Augustine,

summarizing Pelagius's devotee, Celestius, puts it straightforwardly and, I believe, fairly:

> Adam was created mortal, and would have died whether
> he had sinned or not sinned; that Adam's sin injured only
> himself and not the human race; that the law no less than
> the gospel leads us to the kingdom; that there were sin-
> less men previous to the coming of Christ; that new-born
> infants are in the same condition as Adam was before
> the fall; that the whole human race does not, on the one
> hand, die through Adam's death or transgression, nor, on
> the other hand, does the whole human race rise again
> through the resurrection of Christ. ... That a man is able
> to be without sin if he wishes. That infants, even if they
> die unbaptized, have eternal life. That rich men, even if
> they are baptized, unless they renounce all, have, whatever
> good they may seem to have done, nothing of it reckoned
> to them; neither can they possess the kingdom of God.[16]

In this reading, the notion that sin was some sort of inherited condition from which humanity needed to be rescued—a
spiritual death from which they needed to be raised *before* they
could freely cooperate with grace—smacked too much of the
gnostic and pagan fatalism that marked the philosophers and
astrologers of an earlier era.

Pelagius was an optimist with respect to human beings;
Augustine was not so much a pessimist as he was a realist. As

he surveyed the world around him and the world within him, he could not bring himself to agree with Pelagius's notion that human beings were born morally neutral, that Adam's sin was his alone even as Christ's resurrection was Christ's alone, and that we forsake Adam's bad example and imitate Christ's good one, if not by our own efforts exclusively, at least by our own initiation, with our own work leading the way. On the contrary, Augustine's reading of Paul coupled with his pastoral experience and indeed his own past led him in a very different direction. Human beings are enslaved to sin from the moment of their first appearance. Adam's sin, both its guilt and its consequences, were passed on like a disease from parents to children.

It was the pastoral question raised by Christians having children that finally decided the matter. By the fifth century, the accepted practice of baptism included infants. Pelagius and his followers held that infants were without sin—they were like Adam before the fall. Why, then, mused Augustine, did the Pelagians continue to affirm infant baptism? Why does a baby without sin need to be baptized? It is not enough to say, as Pelagius did, that to do otherwise would refuse heaven to the innocent. If a baby truly *is* innocent, then baptism is not necessary. Pelagius's acceptance of the practice could not be made to square with his theology. Augustine put the matter bluntly: "What we are discussing concerns the obliteration of original sin in infants. Let him [Pelagius] clear himself on this point, since he refuses to acknowledge that there is anything in infants which the laver of regeneration has to cleanse."[17]

With the Scriptures, church practice, and pastoral and personal psychology apparently on his side, Augustine's position on original sin won the day—sort of. In the short run, Pelagius was condemned. In the longer run, the Western church did not adopt Augustinianism uncritically, not least because it seemed to lead to a notion of absolute predestination that did in fact deny the universal saving will of God as attested in Scripture (2 Pet 3:9). But the notion that grace preceded all human effort, and that all human beings from babies onward were condemned in Adam and in need of gracious intervention before they could will the good, did become the accepted doctrine of the Western church.

What is sin? What is grace? What does it mean to be a sinner? What does it mean to be human? Don't allow the fact that the matter was addressed through the then-accepted practice of infant baptism distract you. These are fundamental questions that penetrate the particularities of sacramental theology and practice. And it's my conclusion that once the gospel has been exchanged for a political program, the Pelagian answers to those questions are the ones given.

Till We Shall Build Jerusalem

In the darkest days of World War I, the British poet laureate, Robert Bridges, asked Hubert Parry to set a mostly forgotten poem, written just over a century before by William Blake, to music. Bridges hoped that such songs would inspire patriotism and courage in the midst of a war whose outcome was still unclear. So 1916 saw the publication of Parry's setting of the poem. Today, it has become the unofficial English national anthem—at the insistence of King George V, no less. Blake had originally published it in 1808, with the first line as the title. We now know it as "Jerusalem." In full, it reads:

And did those feet in ancient time
Walk upon England's mountains green?
And was the holy Lamb of God
On England's pleasant pastures seen?

And did the Countenance Divine
Shine forth upon our clouded hills?
And was Jerusalem builded here
Among these dark satanic mills?

Bring me my bow of burning gold!
Bring me my arrows of desire!
Bring me my spear! O clouds, unfold!
Bring me my chariot of fire!

I will not cease from mental fight,
Nor shall my sword sleep in my hand,
Till we have built Jerusalem
In England's green and pleasant land.[18]

The first stanza calls on part of the English Holy Grail myth that the child Jesus visited the southwest of England with his uncle (or great uncle) Joseph of Arimathea on a trading voyage.[19] It asks, did it really happen? The second stanza, also constructed as two questions, suggests that even if it did happen, it was of no consequence. For Jerusalem was not "builded here"; "dark satanic mills" were set up instead. While many naturally think of the industrial England of Blake's time, a country whose newly expanding urban centers belched choking fumes from coal-fired factories, I am persuaded that Blake (a religious nonconformist) also has the spires of the Church of England in mind.[20] The mills exploited the new working class while the church worked to keep them in their place: both can be seen behind the words. Either way, the first attempt to build Jerusalem had failed. Thus Blake commits wealth ("my bow of burning gold") and energy ("my arrows of desire") to cooperate militantly ("my spear") with the divine power ("my chariot of fire"—see 2 Kings 2:11) in the cause of social betterment. It is a battle both internal ("mental fight") and external ("my sword ... in my hand") that will persist until he, with likeminded others, has built Jerusalem in England's "green and pleasant land." The poem is aptly summarized by theologian Christopher Rowland this way: "All people, inside and outside the churches ... have the responsibility to attend to the energetic activity of the divine spirit in creation, in history, and in human experience."[21]

The sort of activism inscribed by Blake is close to the core of what it means to be an evangelical Christian. It's one of the Bebbington Quadrilateral's nodes. Evangelicals are moral reformers and have been at least since the Wesleyan revival of the eighteenth century. Would the transatlantic slave trade have been abolished in 1807, and slavery outlawed in the British Empire in 1834, without the preaching of John Wesley in the late eighteenth century and the accompanying activism of William Wilberforce and the Clapham Sect? Maybe, but that's not what happened. The slave trade was outlawed and slavery was abolished because of the activism of people who were regarded by more genteel members of the established church as "religious enthusiasts." And that evangelical activism continues in all kinds of ways in all kinds of places today. It is to be commended.

But in North America in particular it seems that evangelical activism has been severed from its roots in the crucicentric, conversionist preaching of the gospel. I alluded above to the Canadian clinical psychologist Jordan Peterson. There is much about his message that is commendable. His call to responsibility, duty, honor, self-reliance, and self-mastery resonate with many evangelicals, especially those who tilt toward the political right. His willingness to engage in what earlier generations of Christians might have called "the moral sense" of the Bible, reminding us of the depths in our own book, rightly shames those of us who see in the Old Testament only "timeless truths" or bloodthirsty battles and outmoded social mores better set aside. Unlike Pelagius (or at least Pelagianism), Peterson has a deeper sense of the truly tragic nature of the human condition apart from grace.

The most that believing Christians can give Peterson, though, is two cheers. His message, while potent and in many ways helpful (especially to young men), is not the gospel. Why do so many conservative evangelicals embrace his neo-Pelagian vision uncritically? Is it because we no longer know or believe the gospel, including the bad news about the human condition? I think it's actually worse. We know enough of the gospel to see elements of it in Peterson and celebrate them, but not nearly enough to see that Peterson's *Twelve Rules for Life* are not only not the gospel but are at points something quite different.

At the progressive end of the evangelical movement, a similar rootlessness, essentially Pelagian, is much less modest. At best we are animated by a vision of God's kingdom of justice and peace. At worst, enamored with our own capacity to build that kingdom, we refuse to learn the lessons of the failed utopian vision of the twentieth century, and we have forgotten the words of Jesus—his kingdom is not of this world (John 18:36). This does not mean that quietism or some sort of Anabaptist withdrawal is the answer. Rather, we would do well to read *Rerum Novarum*—the foundational doctrine of Catholic social teaching—to see what a Christian social vision unencumbered by the ideologies of our own day actually looks like.[22] Then perhaps we can have a conversation about witnessing to the kingdom's coming rather than erecting it.

When it comes to human nature, we have to say what we see. What we see in the moral self-improvement of the evangelical right and the social transformation of the evangelical left is a false and finally Pelagian gospel that expects us to bootstrap our own moral and social perfection. It is a grace that accompanies us only, not one that actually raises us to life. The fatal flaw with these two visions—far more similar than their adherents appreciate—is that of Pelagius. Both rest on a dubious optimism about human nature. In the words of a later Augustinian theologian, they have yet to account for the awful weight of sin.[23] But like Pelagius, they have both the Scriptures and experience against them. While it may be true that the Augustinian version of original sin cannot be read off the pages of holy writ, it is also true that the church, both East and West, has at least tilted more toward it than the Pelagian alternative. We sin because we are fallen and need to redeemed, imprisoned and need to be rescued, dead and need to be raised. Only afterward does cooperation with grace enter the picture. As for experience, we need only to scroll social media to see—really see—what Chesterton meant when he wrote that sin was as practical as potatoes. It is so immediate to us as to be, well, the ordinary way of things. And that is why the Augustinian vision, in general if not always in the particulars, wins.

Pelagianism's Solution: Reclaiming the Gospel

If ever there were a saintly heretic, it was Pelagius. He was zealous for holiness and urged people to pursue it—apparently with some success. But whether he himself worked out the theology that underlay his exhortations or left it to his followers, that theology was found to be deficient.

Why? Because it did not say what it saw. It presumed a human being who did not in fact finally exist: the morally neutral man or woman who, having pulled themselves out of their sinful habits using the handle of their own righteousness, could walk, albeit with some help, into heaven. Augustine, on the other hand, had a better grasp of human nature. So, for that matter, did the pagan determinists. Human beings are who we are. We are fated. But our doom is not set in the stars, nor is it to be found in our genes or determined by some other mechanical law. Here's the human condition, as old as Adam and as fresh as tomorrow's news: we sin because we're sinners. If we're going to stop sinning, grace has to come first. Grace must raise us to new life, grace must unshackle the will, grace must reorder disordered desire *before* we can cooperate with it in the working out of our sanctification. Augustine saw that what had been true in his own conversion was true for the whole human race. Apart from disruptive, extrinsic, intervening grace, we are lost.

The temptation to build the kingdom on our own, which I have called Pelagianism, has become far too attractive to many politically engaged evangelicals, whether we tilt to the right or the left. If so, the next step is repentance, a twofold movement that turns away from sin, death, and the devil and turns toward grace, the divine life, and God. What does repentance from Pelagianism look like?

Consider these familiar words from the psalmist: "Put not your trust in princes, in a son of man, in whom there is no salvation. When his breath departs, he returns to the earth; on that very day his plans perish" (Ps 146:3–4). Evangelical Pelagianism is at its core a naive trust in those the psalmist calls "princes"— that is, our political class. Let's set aside the charges and counter-charges of corruption, crimes, and nasty behavior that dominate our headlines and just consider what the psalmist says. Our politicians are unfairly, unwisely, and even unkindly burdened with our ultimate trust, not because they are wicked but because they are human. Perhaps this strikes you as obvious, but it cannot be underemphasized. If we inadvertently alter the psalmist's caution to something like, "Put not your trust in *that* prince, for he is wicked," we have not faced the problem fully. We will have left open the possibility that our ultimate trust will be worthily laid at the feet of *our* prince, and once our guy (or gal) is in charge, then everything will be better. This misreading is, in our current climate, perfectly understandable. But it is wrong. It is cover for the Pelagian that lurks within each of us, who says in his heart, "Their guy can't build the kingdom. But ours can." The psalmist advises us to withhold from them the trust proper only to God, especially when they seem to demand it more and more, because they are human beings. They are mortal. They will lose an election. They will die. And when they do, their plans will be undone. They will not deliver the kingdom. Repentance means leaving the temptation to ultimate investment in human structures behind.

Let's consider the next question. In the context of our political Pelagianism, what does repentance as turning to God look like? Back to the psalm: "Blessed is he whose help is the God of Jacob, whose hope is in the LORD his God, who made heaven and earth, the sea, and all that is in them, who keeps faith forever; who executes justice for the oppressed, who gives food to the hungry" (Ps 146:5–7). Already I can hear the scoffing. Isn't this naive quietism? Isn't this withdrawing from society? Well, possibly. But it need not be. On the contrary, it brings us to a hardnosed realism with respect to our leaders and a freeing and joyful confidence when it comes to our God. Our voting options are limited to people. We cannot vote for God, or by our votes or other forms of engagement bring in God's kingdom. We can, however, pray for our leaders, work within our own spheres of influence, however imperfectly, to bear witness to God's kingdom, and bring the good news to people who are often largely inoculated to it.

Conclusion

A final word for that most important activity: bringing the good news to the world. I sometimes wonder if our collective obsession with politics masks a lack of confidence in the gospel as God's own chosen means by which he will convert sinners. Perhaps part of our repentance is a rejection of eloquence and frenetic activity for the sake of the "foolishness of preaching" and confidence in Christ and him crucified (1 Cor 1:18; 2:2). The gospel is foolishness to the Greeks.[24] It was when Paul first brought it to Athens (Acts 17), and it remains so now. But even as he tailored his preaching to his audience, Paul never failed to make the public announcement that God (publicly) raised Christ from the dead and that this event had begun the remaking of the world. That event is the sign of the coming of God's kingdom and the basis for our confidence. If we have lost our nerve and lapsed in our trust in the God who raises the dead, then politics is all we have left. And if politics is all we have left, God help us all. We are above all people most pitiable.

Chapter 6

DONATISM

We're Right; You're Evil

I think almost all the crimes which Christians have perpetrated against each other arise from this, that religion is confused with politics. For, above all other spheres of human life, the Devil claims politics for his own, as almost the citadel of his power. Let us, however, with mutual prayers pray with all our power for that charity which "covers a multitude of sins."

C. S. Lewis, *The Collected Letters of C. S. Lewis*

S o far we've met a magician who was either not-quite-converted or backslid into apostasy; teachers who were so eager to introduce their friends to Jesus that they absorbed him into the prevailing thought patterns of their day; a priest who, though often wrongly portrayed as a denier of the divinity of Christ, was trying to make metaphysical sense of the Bible's presentation of Jesus; and a monk who wanted his spiritual directees to pursue that holiness without which no one shall see the Lord (Heb 12:14). Simon, Valentinus and Cerinthus, Arius, and Pelagius were people who, at least by their own lights, really loved Jesus and sought to speak, live, and teach the truth about him. As such they are worthy of sympathy. In so many sterile presentations of church history, they are merely ciphers for and symbols of error. They are the two dimensional, black-hatted villains against whom the apostles and their orthodox descendants demonstrate their theological brilliance and moral virtue.

But that just isn't true.[1] If I am to allege—as I do—that late modern evangelicals too often tilt toward heresy because of an idolatrous politics, I hope I have not fallen into the trap of casting my opponents as bad people. Sinners? Certainly! But no more than I am. Heretics? Absolutely! But heretics who, like all heretics, force the church to clarify, deepen, and develop sound doctrine. Indeed, these heretics continue to provide me at least with ample material for self-examination. If they are false teachers whose false teachings have been and must continue to be rejected, they are also astringents in my own pursuit of holiness.

This tension—recognizing the heretics' cohumanity as fellow sinners in desperate need of rescue and treating them with as much sympathy as possible, even as we reject their teaching that ultimately steers souls to hell—is near the heart of Christianity. And this tension is especially sharp when we meet our last group, the North African Christians known as the Donatists. As the survivors and descendants of the severest persecutions of the pre-Constantinian era, the Donatists were legitimately angry at those who had recanted the faith under persecution and then sought to be readmitted not simply to church but even to positions of leadership—and worse, that such appeals were often successful.

I can hear their anguished complaints. Can't you? How can I receive the body and blood of the Lord from you, who previously blasphemed his name and forsook his flock, when I lost my status, my occupation, and my family and still stayed faithful? How can I hand over my child to be baptized by you, who handed over the Scriptures to the flames? You mock my sacrifice. You belittle my faithfulness. Your cowardice is rewarded with mitre, cope, and crozier. How dare you! Perhaps especially of all the people I've presented so far, we ought to be cheering for the Donatists. They stand for faithfulness. They stand for courage. They stand for visible holiness.

The Donatists of the Fifth Century

The roots of the fifth-century Donatist controversy were pastoral rather than speculative. Those roots were deep, having been put down during the persecutions of the previous two centuries. Their strength was directly proportional to that of the violence North African churches had endured and the trauma it created in subsequent generations. The image of the faithful church enduring under centuries of severe, unrelenting opposition has been rightly supplanted by a more nuanced picture. Prior to the fourth century, Roman persecution of Christians was regional or local rather than empire-wide, sporadic rather than constant, and more intense in some places than others. If persecution was relatively rare and light in, for example, Gaul and Britain, for Christians in North Africa it was both more frequent and more intense. It was the experience of persecution and some of the responses to it that provoked the heresy.

One very violent persecution occurred in the middle of the third century. When this terrible time ended and Christians could once again emerge, the question of how to respond to those whose faith had lapsed during the terror was especially fraught. Mercy might dictate that in the face of torture or execution, a fall was understandable and, after a period of repentance, forgivable. But the extension of such mercy should not be so lenient as to communicate to those who had remained faithful that their sacrifice had been in vain. Prior to his own martyrdom, Cyprian of Carthage defended his episcopal authority on these matters against Christians in his own diocese who wanted to assign the pastoral task of readmission (or not) to those they dubbed "the confessors," that is, those who had persevered for the faith and survived in the face of prison and worse. The confessors uniquely earned the privilege and responsibility to guard readmission to the church. Fortunately, it seems that the confessors leaned toward mercy, and the matter diminished over time.

This is not to say, however, that it was resolved. When persecution began again in AD 303 under Diocletian, the question reemerged with fresh urgency. Enacted by imperial decree, this last great persecution of the early church was novel insofar as it truly was empire-wide and lengthy—lasting a decade. Like previous persecutions, however, it varied in enforcement and severity from place to place and time to time. North Africa sadly continued in its tradition of particularly severe persecution. Many people recanted to varying degrees. According to church historian Justo González,

> Some bishops avoided further persecution by handing over to the authorities heretical books, and leading them to believe that these were Christian scriptures. Others turned in the genuine scriptures, claiming that in so doing they were avoiding bloodshed, and that this was their responsibility as pastors. Many, both clergy and lay, succumbed to imperial pressure and worshiped the pagan gods—indeed, the number of the latter was such that some chroniclers state that there were days when the pagan temples were full to overflowing.[2]

At the same time, many other Christians remained faithful. Some of these were imprisoned; others, like Origen, were tortured and later died from their injuries; still others, like Cyprian himself, followed Stephen in the path of faithfulness unto death. Although the persecution ended officially with Constantine's Edict of Milan in 313, it seems to have petered out in North Africa several years before that. At that time, the question of how to respond to those who lapsed and wished to return—how to balance faithfulness and mercy—again emerged. González observes that this time around, the confessors tilted away from mercy and toward rigor. If those who handed over heretical books were to be judged generously, the same could not be said for those who handed over the true Scriptures or who worshiped pagan gods. These were dubbed "*traditores*"—traitors, literally, "those who handed over." A word heretofore reserved for Judas Iscariot, no other title could communicate the confessors' contempt or the unremitting nature of the judgment some of them deemed necessary.[3]

It was into this tinderbox that one lit match was tossed. The election of Caecilian to the see of Carthage in 311 ignited the Donatist schism. In a tactic all too familiar to us today, charges of stolen elections and rigged voting were tossed back and forth in attempts both to invalidate the election and to quell dissent. Neither side could convince the other to concede. Instead, Caecilian's unsatisfied opponents elected their own candidate, Majorinus, and after his death, Donatus. Two bishops, one diocese: who was the true bishop of Carthage? Urban

Carthaginians and most of the bishops outside North Africa rallied to Caecilian's side. In the diocese's countryside, outside Carthage proper, Majorinus and Donatus were regarded favorably (indeed, Donatus would remain bishop of the rival church for the next fifty years, and eventually the movement was given his name).

But why was there controversy in the first place? Here church politics and ecclesiology blur each into the other. Familiar dynamics were at work: deeply rooted rivalries between urban centers and rural communities matched the mutual suspicion between the Italian upper class and native North African, Berber farmers. Race, class, and wealth were the major sociopolitical points of conflict that ensured the depth and longevity of the Donatist controversy.

Here, however, we're focused on the theology that was deployed. The Donatists traced their ecclesial family tree to those third-century confessors who sought to circumscribe the participation of former *traditores* in church life, if not exclude them altogether. Upon hearing that one of the three bishops who laid hands on Caecilian to consecrate him was a *traditor*, they had had enough of the tradition of leniency. Though Caecilian's supporters denied the charge, it stuck ... enough. Furthermore, the Donatists insisted, the other bishops who had joined in the consecration did so knowing full well the indictment against him and participated anyway. They were complicit. Caecilian's rigorist enemies reasoned that the presence of the *traditor* with the knowledge of the other bishops invalidated his consecration.

The sinfulness of the bishops placed them outside the true church and so rendered them unable to serve sacramentally. Caecilian wasn't a rival bishop to Majorinus or Donatus because he wasn't a bishop at all.

And the problem, the Donatists said, was not limited to Caecilian, the supposed *traditor* who consecrated him, or the other two bishops who acted in concert with them. Like a contagion, their sin spread to infect those who approved of their actions. As a result, the Donatists argued, any ordinations or sacramental administrations conducted by these men and their supporters were also invalid. Any priests they ordained were false priests, the bread and wine they consecrated were not the body and blood of Jesus, and the waters they exorcized and blessed did not actually baptize. In those invalidly ordained priests, the episcopal line to the apostles was broken. Because they were not holy, neither were they one, catholic, or apostolic. They led a false church, presided over fake sacraments, and mediated no grace. The true church, the pure and holy bride of Christ, was led only by those who had remained faithful.

Given the long North African experience of persecution, made all the more painful by the class dynamics of the Italian oppressors and the Berber victims, the seemingly genuine holiness of the early Donatists was potent. The tear in the fabric of the Christian communion in North Africa was quick, severe, and apparently permanent. Catholic Christianity in North Africa was little more than a handful of urban enclaves surrounded by flourishing Donatist communities. So when Augustine finally entered the fray in the early fifth century, the catholic church was actually the minority body in Christian North Africa.

Enter Augustine, Again

In the creed, Augustine and his Donatist opponents together confessed their belief in one, holy, catholic, and apostolic church. For both, the true church was unified, set apart, universal, and descended from the apostles. They parted, however, over the four marks' interrelationship. For the Donatists, the church is one, catholic, and apostolic only insofar as she is first a holy church, a communion of saints, the pure bride of Christ. The church that bore the marks of unity, catholicity, and apostolicity is that body whose leaders remained faithful under trial and overcame: the Donatist church. Likewise, a body whose leaders are demonstrably unholy—as the rehabilitated *traditores* and their supporters so obviously were—has left the one church behind and, having done so, forfeited any claims to being universal (catholic) or descended from Christ's first followers (apostolic). The practical outworking of this insistence was sacramental: only the true, holy church had sacraments that effected grace. The sin of apostasy, having placed the *traditores* outside that church, had rendered their sacraments and their successors null and void. "There could be no fellowship between the church of Christ [the Donatists] and the synagogue of Satan."[4]

Ever the pastor, Augustine engaged the Donatists precisely at this point of sacramental practice—and especially baptism, for it was here that the consequences of the peculiar Donatist emphasis on holiness impinged most upon the lives of ordinary Christians. Like today, ordinary believers were largely uninterested in academic arguments about predestination, the relationship between grace and sanctification, or the nature of the church. "Was my child saved at her baptism?" and "Was I?" on the other hand, were questions everyone could grasp. That was the point on which Augustine made his stand.

By the time Augustine entered the anti-Donatist fray just after the turn of the fifth century, the two rival churches had struggled side by side for one hundred years. The original antagonists were long gone. This meant that, as far as the Donatists were concerned, no catholic baptisms were valid. Accordingly, any catholic who entered a Donatist community had to be baptized (not rebaptized, since according to the Donatists their first baptism hadn't been a baptism but just spilled water). The catholics, by contrast, were more generous. They did not rebaptize Donatists who switched communions, but recognized their rivals' baptism as valid. The catholics, we might say, earned their name by embracing the opponents who excluded them.

To understand this significant difference in practice, we must begin with a disagreement about the church's holiness. Augustine and the Donatists each confessed belief in the holy church, but they defined that holiness differently. According to Augustine, the holiness that marks the church is Christ's own holiness, freely given to the church in her sacraments. The church is holy because she belongs to Jesus. Holiness is an objective, present reality that both animates the lives of believers on their way to sainthood and exists alongside the sinfulness of the church's members, including those in leadership. It is a forever-offered gift of grace that is sometimes imperfectly accepted and sometimes spurned. According to the Donatists, on the other hand, the church's holiness is entirely the holiness of its members. It is the purity, faithfulness, courage, and sanctification of her people. If anyone lapses in their pursuit of perfection, they are by that action put outside the church, and if they are outside the church, they are unable to welcome anyone into it sacramentally.

From the Donatist definition of holiness, their understanding of baptism (and all the sacraments) inevitably follows. The sacraments are the means of grace exclusively *inside* the church. If a priest's lack of holiness has placed him outside the church, then the sacrament he celebrated wasn't really a sacrament. The efficacy of the sacrament was dependent on the worthiness and holiness of the celebrant, such that saving grace could be impeded by the celebrant's sin. Augustine pointed out the inevitable and unhappy pastoral consequence: if that is true, then, because they had no access to the heart or conscience of the celebrant, no one could ever know truly if they had really been baptized, if they had really been saved at the font. Augustine puts it this way:

> But how, again, shall they have any certainty about the good who are to give them faith, if what we look to is the conscience of the giver, which is unseen by the eyes of the proposed recipient? Therefore, according to their judgment, the salvation of the spirit is made uncertain,

so long as in opposition to the holy Scriptures, which say, "It is better to trust in the Lord than to put confidence in man," and, "Cursed be the man that trusteth in man," they remove the hope of those who are to be baptized from the Lord their God, and persuade them that it should be placed in man; the practical result of which is, that their salvation becomes not merely uncertain, but actually null and void. For "salvation belongeth unto the Lord," and "vain is the help of man." Therefore, whosoever places his trust in man, even in one whom he knows to be just and innocent, is accursed. Whence also the Apostle Paul finds fault with those who said they were of Paul saying, "Was Paul crucified for you? or were ye baptized in the name of Paul?"[5]

This was not to say that Augustine shelved church discipline—far from it! In the same work, Augustine points to discipline rightly exercised on catholic leaders who had engaged in grave sin.[6] Rather, his point was that the sins of the clergy did not invalidate the sacraments they administered. The sacraments were enlivened not by the clergy's personal holiness but by God's grace active in the church and even outside it. Baptism could not be undone or impaired by the sins of the celebrant because baptism "is Christ's, by whomsoever it be given."[7] The holiness of the church that we confess as a matter of faith is Christ's own holiness. The grace that works in the sacraments is God's own grace. Thus, because both the catholics and the Donatists baptized with water in the name of God—Father, Son, and Holy Spirit—the catholics could and did accept baptism performed by the Donatists as valid, even as the Donatists refused to reciprocate.

This leads us finally to contrary understandings of the nature of the church. For the Donatists, the church's holiness was visible and alive in the lives of her members. Accordingly, lives that lacked such holiness weren't actually members. Because the church truly was the *ekklesia*, the community that had been *called out* from the world by the very voice of God, it was the community's responsibility to expel those who had lapsed (perhaps permanently, depending on the severity of the fall). Augustine countered that the holiness the Donatists expected to see, which was the basis for their adjudication, was not always evident to them. On the contrary, it was hidden in the predestining work of God and would only be revealed at the end of days. Until then, instead of a pure body, the church would be a mixed body of sinners, some on their way to sainthood and others not. Wheat and tares would grow together until the final revelation of the sons and daughters of God at the last day. This is not to say that Augustine identified the true church with the invisible church, as some later Reformers might have done. It is simply to reiterate that prior to Christ's second coming, the church's holiness is the holiness of Christ mediated through the sacraments. It is always present and visible there, even if it is at best imperfectly present and at worst entirely lacking among the church's members. Discipline should be exercised, certainly, but cautiously and generously, because the final judgment rests ultimately with God.

Close to Home

"Which baptism saves?" is hardly an animating pastoral question
for contemporary North American evangelicals. Those evangelicals who tilt toward a sacramental view of salvation consider the
matter settled: Augustine was (mostly) right. The efficacy of the
sacrament hinges on the presence of God's grace by word and
Spirit, not on the holiness of the minister. Evangelicals from free
churches likely don't understand baptism sacramentally at all, so
the question never arises. If baptism is about my declaration of
allegiance to Jesus, the piety of the president doesn't enter the
picture. The nature of baptismal regeneration is a rarefied issue,
of interest only to history nerds.

But let's not get sidetracked by the immediate pastoral matter
through which Augustine came to the Donatist controversy.
Master rhetorician that he was, he was dressing a significant
theological problem in garb that would appeal to the people he
wanted to convince: not so much the Donatist leaders, whose orientation on the issue was fixed, as their (and his own) followers,
who may have been posing these sorts of questions. Is there a pastoral question that may animate evangelicals through which the
same theological issue might be addressed today? Let's replace
"Which baptism saves?" with a similarly pastoral (but decidedly
unsacramental) question, one that will bring the Donatist controversy perhaps a little too close to home: "How close to the
world is too close?" Here is a pastoral issue that has been at the
heart of evangelicalism ever since Carl Henry published *Uneasy
Conscience* in 1947, initiating the split with fundamentalism.

Let me explain. The late nineteenth and early twentieth centuries saw the fracturing of establishment Christianity in North America. The presenting issues included the teaching of higher biblical criticism and liberal theology in denominational seminaries and the teaching of the theory of evolution in public schools. Denominational leaders, seminaries, and local churches divided over whether or just how much these cultural and academic changes could be accommodated.[8] In the split, say, between Princeton and Westminster Seminaries, the theological issues were cast in the language of the theological academy: Who had the better arguments? In the pews, the issue eventually became a moral one: Who had compromised with the world? Differing answers to that moral question marked the slow separation of neoevangelicals (now just evangelicals) from fundamentalists, starting around 1941. By 1960, when the fissures between fundamentalism proper and neoevangelicalism were fixed, the debate was about the nature of the holiness of the true Church.[9]

For evangelicals, that deliberation has continued to this day as a boundary-defining matter. At one edge, we define ourselves against the strict separationism of our fundamentalist parents and grandparents by insisting that we ought to engage the culture and that the gospel ought to be relevant to seekers. At the other, this perceived need for engagement stands in tension with the equally evangelical conviction that evangelism is, at bottom, a call to conversion—to radical change. Some seekers ought, with the grace of God, to become disciples, and that will mean leaving some patterns of thought and behavior behind. Just where is the dividing line between cultural engagement and cultural accommodation? Put theologically, what does a holy church—a church unstained by the world—look like?

The Donatist question may be as old as the fourth century, but it is as fresh as the twenty-first. The Donatist question still animates evangelicals across the political spectrum. What behavior is genuinely holy behavior, to be cultivated regardless of cultural acceptance, and what is just our own peculiar sanctimony, once defining but now obsolete? But the varying forms of the question and the various definitions of worldliness are not what interests me. What does interest me is the quick recourse to moral judgment. In the past, the provoking issues might have been biblical (who wrote the Pentateuch?), theological (is atonement substitutionary?), or moral (can a Christian drink?). There was always a holiness component to the answer. To be "unstained by the world" (Jas 1:27) involved, in part, having the "right" answers to these questions. Today, on the other hand, the issues are increasingly political. Do you have the right views on climate change? Global poverty? Human sexuality? And while it might be familiar for the evangelical right to trot out these tropes, its members are hardly alone in doing so. Disagree with certain members of the evangelical right or left on any of these hot-button issues, and you will find an old fundamentalist preacher ready to be unleashed.

A Solution to Evangelical Donatism?

If this debate has been with us since the beginning, why does it matter today? Because today, perhaps more than ever before, to have the wrong answer on these political questions is not simply to be mistaken. It is to be morally suspect. It is to be unholy. And where previous generations might have moved from disagreement to an old-fashioned altar call and a plea for repentance and reconciliation, modern evangelicals seem to move straight to exclusion.

Ironically, furthermore, these are often matters on which the Bible has nothing to say, at least directly. The Bible is quite clear on chastity before marriage and fidelity after, but it does not speak with the same clarity on how best to respond to gender dysphoria. Similarly, while the Bible places human beings at the center of God's creation, created in God's image and charged with representing him by tending and expanding what he has made, it says nothing whatever about CO_2 levels or fossil fuels. Does the Bible speak to these? Certainly. But discerning just what the Bible says is a matter of prudential judgment.

And the biblical answers to at least some of these questions are bound by historical and contextual factors and may in fact change over time and geography. For example, if purchasing an electric car actually increases one's personal carbon footprint (because it is dependent on carbon-intense means of extraction of its constituent components and requires extensive modification of urban infrastructures), it may be the prudential judgment of biblically sound environmental stewardship to stick with a gasoline engine. Or, perhaps more complicatedly, if our national commitment to renewable energy sources forces many of the world's poor to burn biomass, dung, and other materials that will increase disease and keep them poor, maybe we need to reexamine the global rush to renewable energy for good biblical reasons—namely, care for the poorest of the poor. And if our opponents on these questions can be written out of the conversation by labeling them climate deniers or evil globalists, we don't actually have to listen to a position that may compel us to modify ours. We are right and virtuous; they are wrong and evil. The solution is not to listen; the solution is to compel them to shut up, lest they persuade people with misinformation.

Donatism is rejected and renounced by a twofold strategy. First, by the deliberate withholding of judgment on people in disagreement. It is the strategy I have employed in this book, in my attempt to disentangle the classical heretics from their positions and to present both in as charitable a light as possible. Jesus's call to withhold judgment seems to me especially applicable here. It is not for me to condemn or acquit Simon, Cerinthus, Arius, Pelagius, or Donatus any more than those brothers and sisters with whom I stand in sometimes sharp disagreement. It is a matter of *my* discipleship to a crucified Savior that I do not condemn, that I seek reconciliation when possible, and that my first instinct at the personal level is to mercy. If I seek that for myself when standing in God's presence, it is incumbent on me to cultivate that same orientation when standing in the presence of my fellow disciples. The responsibility for final judgment lies exclusively with God.

Second, we reject Donatism by an equally deliberate commitment to the investigation and, if necessary, condemnation of wrong ideas. Patience and prudence do not demand a continuous forestalling of conclusions. To say that Simon, Cerinthus, Arius, Pelagius, Donatus, or their contemporary inheritors are subject to the judgment of God alone is not to say that churches ought to affirm their ideas. If heresy means anything at all, it means that some ideas are no longer up for discussion. And where heresies continue to be found, they ought to be exposed and rejected, even as we call those who hold them to the same repentance that (hopefully) defines our own discipleship. The rejection of false ideas in the pursuit of truth is part and parcel of being the church in history; it is the task of faith seeking understanding, of faith and reason working together in the pursuit of him who is the Truth.[10]

But precisely here we run into what might look like evangelicalism's Achilles' heel: the seeming lack of an agreed-upon authority that can end the debate. Augustine may well have abided by the dictum, "Roma locuta est, causa finitum est" ("Rome has spoken, the matter is over"), but there is no such solution for us. There is no Grand Rapids or Chicagoland head office that can address heresy in a full and final way. Of course, while some evangelicals may look longingly across the Tiber for someone to provide this authority, Rome's structures don't seem to work well in practice, either: silenced priests and theologians seem to be quite popular these days, as do bishops and cardinals who openly deny accepted Roman Catholic teaching. The Roman institutions that exist to address these problems seem strangely powerless to stop them. But if Rome is too restrained or lacks the will to pull the levers at its disposal, we are in the less enviable position of lacking the levers altogether.

Is this lack really a fatal weakness, though? Anglican theologian Oliver O'Donovan insists that the Church has only the authority to persuade; when it gets itself mixed up in the authority given by God to the magistrate, namely, the authority to compel, there is no end to the mischief that results.[11] And it is precisely this point that the modern Pelagians and Donatists rightly see in their opponents but ignore in themselves: a willingness to use coercion, if not to silence their opponents, at least to steer them toward a different way of thinking.

The willingness to forsake persuasion for compulsion is not new. In the original Donatist controversy, not even Augustine himself remained immune to this temptation. Though his anti-Donatist writings show that he originally preferred persuasion, the crisis's intractability, coupled with all sorts of escalating shenanigans (including violence on both sides), led him to eventually believe that the state's authority to compel was the only way to resolve it.[12] In a letter to a former friend and catholic-become-Donatist, Vincentius, Augustine marshals a rhetorician's skills and exegetical abilities to justify the use of Roman soldiers to resolve this theological matter. And while a case could perhaps have been made for a limited use of force based on the need for social stability—after all, the Donatists were engaged in violence too—Augustine did not stay there. In his interpretation of the parable of the wedding banquet (Luke 14:16–23), in which the later guests were "compelled" to come in, he seems to be persuading himself as much as he was Vincentius of the rightness of this position. It seems there is no easy way out of this dilemma short of the advent of the Lord. Forsaking persuasion for compulsion to end debate and restore stability may be tempting, but it may also be to forsake the way of the cross.

Conclusion

The sympathy we feel for the Donatists cannot be denied (along with the accompanying discomfort with which we might read the later writings of Augustine). But the Donatists are heretics—indeed, perhaps the most pernicious heretics of all, precisely because their complaint is so obviously just (even if their solution isn't). Their desire to maintain the visible holiness of the church was right; their refusal to readmit recanters or to recognize the sacramental authority of bishops and priests who fell effectively removed God as the final judge. This provoked a division in North African Christianity that was never truly healed. Instead, it was replaced by a deeper one when the Arian Vandals sacked Carthage, and both divisions were rooted out two centuries later by the armies of Islam. We might wonder whether the once-vibrant Christian civilization in North Africa fell so utterly because it had been irreparably weakened by centuries of division.

The lesson of Donatism for late modern evangelicals is this. Once we've convinced ourselves—sometimes with good reason!—that we're the good guys, there's no amount of mischief we won't get up to. Once we're certain that truth, goodness, and beauty lie entirely with us, there is no need to extend respect, regard, or consideration to our opponents. So Donatism follows hard on the heels of Pelagianism, theologically if not chronologically. If we come to believe so fiercely that we are building the kingdom that we will not countenance any criticism of our program, it's all too easy to see our opponents not simply as mistaken, but as evil. And evil must be eradicated. If God's on our side, we'll start the next war.

Chapter 7

ALL THIS I WILL GIVE YOU

Treaties with the Egyptians ... or Worse

Wherever politics tries to be redemptive,
it is promising too much. Where it wishes to do
the work of God, it becomes not divine, but demonic.

Pope Benedict XVI, *Truth and Tolerance*

E vangelicals have been navel gazers from the outset, but we've moved steadily away from the hollers and camp meetings and tent revivals to the center of contemporary culture: megachurches, celebrity pastors, and Ned Flanders. But what fruit has been borne? It's not lacking altogether, but neither is it abundant. And all sides agree that, having finally made it into the elite culture, the culture decided to forsake religion for politics. Not only has the hoped-for "place at the table" disappeared, but so has the furniture and even the house. How do evangelicals fit in this new post-Christian yet deeply religious American moment?

The evangelical right calls us to retrench, to double down on the old alliances that brought us, rightly or wrongly, to prominence through the 1980s. The evangelical left is seeking to forge new alliances with the emerging elite while pouring scorn on previous generations. Each side, I believe, fails to see its mirror image in the other. Each side is hoping to maintain or secure political advantage by selling the gospel to political power brokers who may find us useful, but that's about it. I have called that Simony. This invariably has led to changing the gospel from an announcement of an event, namely, the resurrection of Jesus, to a rhetorical flourish for a political message peddled for other reasons altogether. Jesus is malleable. His gospel can be shaped to fit whatever political needs are at hand.

Jesus is still important, to be sure, but only insofar as he fits what we already believe for other reasons. In short, gnosticism. The good news of salvation soon becomes a message of self-improvement, in which the Savior helps us save ourselves by strengthening our hold on the right politics. A Savior who doesn't save is the Christ of Arianism. Now christless, the political goal is conflated with the kingdom. Not a kingdom that's erupting in our midst, but a kingdom we will build—Pelagianism. And finally, since the kingdom of God is the kingdom we're building, our opponents must not simply be mistaken. They must be evil. Compromise was the art of politics when politics was penultimate. Now that politics are transcendent, compromise is impossible. For all our reluctance to believe in binaries anymore, any political discussion in America will reveal that the old distinctions between good and evil, clean and unclean, sacred and profane are alive and well and have moved from the temple to the state house. In the church, this is the resurgence of Donatism. Whether we're white or woke, I believe this pattern holds.

I've avoided specific examples in this book, lest it seem like I'm speaking from one side to the other. While I have my own convictions (and let's face it, they're pretty clear to anyone who wants to look in these pages), I do believe the indictment includes all of us. Further, I have deliberately cast that indictment as heresy to indicate that it is a spiritual problem first. We will not straighten out our political issues until we're clear that we have gone astray spiritually. The solution is not to switch sides, and still less to carve out a political third way. The solution is to repent, in the sense of the New Testament word *metanoia*. Aided by grace and fueled by godly sorrow for sin, we need to change our minds and our actions. To forsake the broad way that leads to destruction, and search again for the narrow way that leads to life. To cultivate prudence and patience, faithfulness in witness, and a political civility that recognizes the important but secondary place of politics in our lives. Most of all, it means to recover our own language and not scorn our past. It means to learn again what it means to be an evangelical: a poor, wayfaring stranger who holds within her hands a priceless treasure to be shared with the whole world.

Making Deals with the Egyptians

So far, too few of us have taken this route. We feel it is impractical, that it forsakes our public responsibilities, that it is a strategy of withdrawal. I think such charges are not only false but morally culpable. To make them is to know deep down they are untrue. To make them is, indeed, to bear false witness. But the charges are made all the same. Why? Because, like Judah in the days of Sennacherib, we're afraid. And like Judah's leaders, we are casting about for this-worldly help instead of trusting God.

With the Assyrians pressing from the North, region after region falling before their mighty army, Judah was terrified. They would be next. The politically wise strategy in the face of this impending loss of power, identity, and self-understanding was to forge an alliance with Assyria's counterbalance: Egypt. And that is what the leaders of Judah did. God was not pleased.

Speaking through the mouth of his prophet Isaiah, this is what the LORD God said:

> "Ah, stubborn children," declares the LORD,
> "who carry out a plan, but not mine,
>   and who make an alliance, but not of my Spirit,
>   that they may add sin to sin;
>   who set out to go down to Egypt,
>   without asking for my direction,
>   to take refuge in the protection of Pharaoh
>   and to seek shelter in the shadow of Egypt!
> Therefore shall the protection of Pharaoh
>   turn to your shame,
>   and the shelter in the shadow of Egypt to your
>   humiliation.
> For though his officials are at Zoan
>   and his envoys reach Hanes,
> everyone comes to shame
>   through a people that cannot profit them,
> that brings neither help nor profit,
>   but shame and disgrace." (Isa 30:1–5)

The issue was not that seeking alliances was intrinsically wrong. The issue was that this alliance was struck not only with Judah's ancient enemy, but God's, and furthermore it was done without divine consultation or approval. Seeking Egyptian protection was the obvious thing for the smaller, weaker Judah to do, but it was not God's plan for his people. Had they inquired of him, they would have known that, however expedient this plan seemed to be, it would not deliver the intended outcome. Rather than protection from Assyria and economic stability, only shame and disgrace awaited.

God's nickname for Egypt makes the uselessness of the treaty obvious: "Rahab who sits still" (Isa 30:7). Rahab here may be a proper name referring to the ancient sea monster symbolic of anticreative chaos (see Isa 51:9), or it might be a title: "proud one." I suspect both are intended. Egypt is mighty. Egypt is proud. Perhaps, Judah thought, Egypt alone can withstand the steady march of the Assyrian conquerors south and west. But, God says, Egypt is Rahab. Egypt is the physical stand-in for the spiritual enemy from which I delivered you when I brought you through the Red Sea. Egypt is the enemy whose gods I conquered when I set you free. However proud and strong Egypt may appear, to turn to Egypt is to turn away from me and back to my ancient enemy (and yours too!). And Egypt won't deliver. Egypt will sit still. Egypt promises everything, but Egypt will do nothing.

But the people are tired of hearing from God and his prophet:

> For they are a rebellious people,
>   lying children,
> children unwilling to hear
>   the instruction of the LORD;
> who say to the seers, "Do not see,"
>   and to the prophets, "Do not prophesy to us
>   what is right;

speak to us smooth things,

> prophesy illusions,

leave the way, turn aside from the path,

> let us hear no more about the Holy One of Israel."

> > (Isa 30:9–11)

Judah is committed to the path of politics, convinced that the power of Egypt is all that can preserve it from the marauding Assyrians. Even though God through his prophet continues to extend the invitation to trust in him, Judah will have none of it.

For thus said the Lord GOD, the Holy One of Israel,

"In returning and rest you shall be saved;

> in quietness and in trust shall be your strength."

But you were unwilling, and you said,

"No! We will flee upon horses";

> therefore you shall flee away;

and, "We will ride upon swift steeds";

> therefore your pursuers shall be swift. (Isa 30:15–16)

Judah was so consumed by fear and the perceived need for a political solution that they would not accept God's counterintuitive help. Returning? Rest? Quietness? Trust? And sadly, they would live with the consequences: the fear that drove them to Egypt's arms would cause them to flee at just one approaching Assyrian (Isa 30:17).

Does this sound familiar? It does to me. It describes me, all too often. I'm afraid it also describes the more vocal elements of the evangelical movement, right and left, who have surrendered the gospel for the sake of retaining or gaining political power in a situation of cultural decline. Offered God's rest, I am tempted to choose swift horses instead—only to find that my pursuers are swifter. I'm tempted to choose the swift horses, rather than the resources in God's word—resources that would provide God's salvation and strength to endure the most difficult days, even if they won't necessarily ensure ongoing temporal influence.

As this book comes to an end, perhaps it's time for you, dear reader, to ask whether this weakness lies in you, too. In our modern, buffered world, in which the supernatural is safely bracketed out of public life, in which those who think, "The LORD will not do good, nor will he do ill" (Zeph 1:12) are counted wise, in which Christian observance is at best an idiosyncratic hobby and at worst publicly destructive, the temptation to find a more realistic survival strategy is very strong. And if this book has been a cautionary tale about succumbing to it, that is not to say that I am not myself tempted, or that I have not yielded to that temptation at times. As much as I see disturbing trends rooted in heretical casts of mind in contemporary evangelical forays into politics and public life, my only prayer remains, "God, be merciful to me, a sinner!" (Luke 18:13).

In the Ten Commandments (Exod 20; Deut 5), God addresses Israel as an individual, as one who is simultaneously God's adopted son and God's betrothed bride. A nation and people, certainly—but one whose corporate identity is sealed in the heart of each Israelite. The Ten Commandments are given to form God's son, God's bride. They are to form *all* God's children as though they are addressed exclusively to each of them.

In the same way, God addresses his bride, the church, that wild branch grafted into the covenantal olive tree. Recognizing our corporate identity doesn't diminish our individual responsibility. If a heretical politics rooted in the desperate desire to remain relevant has crept into the heart of our movement, it is only because it has crept into the hearts of our people—including my own heart. If and when I succumb to the desire to make a treaty with today's Egyptians, I break the first commandment: "You shall have no other gods before me" (and probably the second commandment too: "You shall not make for yourself a carved image"). And I must repent.

And then what? Do better next time? Well, yes and no. Of course genuine repentance includes the resolve never to commit that sin (now confessed and forgiven) again. But as any pastor worth his or her salt can tell you, the same sins are often repeated, and that doesn't necessarily mean the previous repentance wasn't genuine. It means that the hard work of sanctification, the hard work of continual conversion to the way of Jesus, the hard work of cooperating with grace, takes a long time to make a saint. Our hope does not lie in the vain promise we so often make to God, "I'll do better next time."

In Christ Alone

The story of the Old Testament is the story of the failure of Israel and the stubborn faithfulness of God. And gentiles incorporated into that story find themselves there as well. We reject the Ten Commandments as surely as Israel did. We reject them corporately; we reject them individually. In the Book of Common Prayer, after hearing the Ten Commandments summarized in the commandments to love both God and neighbor, the reality of our desperate state is set before us in the words of a prayer: "Lord have mercy upon us, and write both these thy laws in our hearts, we beseech thee. Lord have mercy upon us. Christ have mercy upon us. Lord have mercy upon us." The Ten Commandments, the lifegiving law of God, are not yet written on our hearts. And until they are, we stand in need of mercy.

The good news of the gospel is that mercy is available, lavish and abundant. It is found in union with the one Israelite who keeps covenant with God, where Israel fails (Jew and gentile together). There is one Israelite who keeps all Ten Commandments all the time; one Israelite who, at the cost of the cross, will keep faith with us until the end. Did Jesus face the temptation to make a treaty with the Egyptians? Was he invited to take the way of political power over the way set forth by his Father in his baptism? Of course he was. It is the last and greatest of the devil's temptations (Matt 4:1–11). Having defeated Satan's appeals to material provision ("turn these stones to bread") and spiritual power ("throw yourself down from the temple"), Jesus faces the tempter's full force: "Again, the devil took him to a very high mountain and showed him all the kingdoms of the world and their glory. And he said to him, 'All these will I give you if you will fall down and worship me'" (Matt 4:8–9). As he has done for each temptation, the incarnate Word resists this last temptation with the written word, this time by combining Deuteronomy 6:13 and 1 Samuel 7:3: "You shall worship the Lord your God and him only shall you serve" (Matt 4:10).

If I were to preach a sermon on this last temptation, I'd develop the following points: (1) The political temptation is a temptation to idolatry—to worship someone other than God. (2) The political temptation makes politics the means of redemption—thereby making a secondary good a primary evil. (3) The political temptation opens politics to the demonic—the kingdoms of this world do in fact in some way belong to the evil one until the last day. And (4) the only resistance is union with Christ and reliance on the word—which is two ways of saying the same thing. The Word is in the words.

In resisting the political temptation to the very end, both in the wilderness and all the way to the cross, Jesus does not only give us an example of how to behave when we are confronted with similar satanic invitations. He certainly does that, but that is not the good news of this passage. It's not the good news because, unlike the Lord, we cannot resist temptation to the very end. We yield. This book has been an extended invitation to see just how and where politically engaged evangelicals have agreed with the enemy. Having given up on the rescue of God (Isa 30:15), we have made a treaty with the Egyptians and, much more gravely, with the satanic horde that lies behind and beneath Egypt's and Assyria's power.

The good news is that the one Israelite—our representative, whether we are Jew or gentile—has borne this temptation to the end. And not only as our representative, but as our substitute. He bears the temptation instead of us. Where we fail, he has succeeded. He has made our failure his in order that we might live in his victory. Where we would make treaties with the powers, both material and immaterial, he continually conquers them by the blood of his cross. Where we have succumbed to heresy, he remains the truth who alone sets us free. We do not need to sell the gospel for relevance, turn it into an ideology, reduce it to moral exemplarism, render it the accomplishment of our own effort, or demonize those who demur. To do so is not fidelity, however much we try to convince ourselves otherwise. It is precisely the opposite. It exposes our own unbelief. And the solution to unbelief always and only is repentance: forsaking our wicked ways and unrighteous thoughts and turning again to the one who alone will "abundantly pardon" (Isa 55:7).

Just as I Am

At the beginning of this book, I invited you to walk the sawdust trail with me to the sound of the old hymn:

> Just as I am without one plea
> But that thy blood was shed for me
> And that thou bidst me come to thee
> O Lamb of God, I come. I come.

I am too quick to sell out for safety, for influence, for the status quo. I am too quick to reduce the gospel to an ideology. I am too quick to reduce the Lord to a cheerleader, to make the kingdom my own project, and to demean the dignity of those who disagree with that vision. I need to bow my knees at the altar, to surrender again to the only one who can truly judge, save, and deliver. I'm not alone. Too many books, too much heated rhetoric, too much of an embrace of what Bishop Robert Barron has called "the culture of contempt" tell me that my failings, my sin, is not solely mine.

> In returning and rest you shall be saved;
> in quietness and trust shall be your strength. (Isa 30:15)

May God find us in Christ. May God find us willing.

> O Lord, I am yours; save me! (Ps 119:94)

ENDNOTES

Prayer

William Laud (1573–1645) wrote this prayer for his *A Summarie of Devotions* (1677). It has been included in Prayers and Thanksgivings since the 1928 Book of Common Prayer.

Chapter 1

1. Carl F. H. Henry, *The Uneasy Conscience of Modern Fundamentalism* (1947; repr., Eerdmans, 2003).
2. Mark A. Noll, *The Scandal of the Evangelical Mind* (Eerdmans, 1995).
3. Albert Schweizer, *The Quest of the Historical Jesus* (1906; repr., Dover, 2005).
4. H. Richard Niebuhr, *Christ and Culture* (Harper Torchbooks, 1951).
5. Constantine is another controversial figure in this tale, whose Christian profession is well beyond the subject of this book. Against those who insist on using *Constantinianism* as a sneer word, Peter Leithart's *Defending Constantine* (InterVarsity Press, 2010) is the strongest rebuttal.
6. The image is from Evelyn Waugh, *Brideshead Revisited: The Sacred and Profane Memories of Captain Charles Ryder* (1945; repr., Penguin Classics, 2023).

7. The radical difference between pre- and post-Christendom, it seems to me, is what many critics of Rod Dreher's *The Benedict Option: A Strategy for Christians in a Post-Christian Nation* (Sentinel, 2017) fail to grasp.

8. See the masterly Tom Holland, *Dominion: How the Christian Revolution Remade the World* (Basic Books, 2019).

9. See Alasdair MacIntyre, *After Virtue* (Duckworth, 1981).

10. On this, see Ross Douthat, *Bad Religion: How We Became a Nation of Heretics* (Free Press, 2013) and Joseph Bottum, *An Anxious Age: The Post-Protestant Ethic and the Spirit of America* (Image, 2014).

11. *The Catechism of the Catholic Church*, second edition (Doubleday, 2003), 2089.

Chapter 2: Simony

1. Tim Perry, "What is Simony?" *Faith Today*, May-June, 2001, 46.

2. See especially Irenaeus, *Against Heresies* 1.23.

3. For a full accounting of the legends and an exhaustive list of primary material, see Alberto Ferreiro, *Simon Magus in Patristic, Medieval and Early Modern Traditions* (Brill, 2005).

4. *Inferno*'s literary setting is AD 1300, three years before Pope Boniface's actual death in 1303.

5. Taylor sums it up this way: "By social imaginary, I mean ... the ways people imagine their social existence, how they fit together with others, how things go on between them and their fellows, the expectations that are normally met and the deeper normative notions and images that underlie these expectations." Charles Taylor, *Modern Social Imaginaries* (Duke University Press, 2004), 23.

6. See Heiko Oberman, *Luther: Man Between God and the Devil* (Harper Collins, 1993).

7. In Taylor's words, the immanent frame is "our familiar picture of the natural, 'physical' universe as governed by exceptionless laws, which may reflect the wisdom and benevolence of the creator, but don't require in order to be understood—or (at least on a first level) explained—any reference to a good aimed at, whether in the form of a Platonic Idea, or of Ideas in the mind of God." Charles Taylor, *A Secular Age* (Belknap Press, 2007), 542.

8. According to Taylor, the buffered self "can see itself as invulnerable, as the master of the meanings of things for it. ... It can form the ambition of disengaging from whatever is beyond the boundary, and of giving its own autonomous order to its life" (Taylor, *Secular Age*, 38–39).

9. Alvin Plantinga, *Warranted Christian Belief* (Oxford University Press, 2000), 173. Plantinga is summarizing here the view of John Calvin on the allegedly inbuilt awareness of the divine—the *sensus divinitatis*—that is the source of all authentic devotion and idolatry. See John Calvin, *Institutes of the Christian Religion* 1.3.

10. C. S. Lewis, *The Four Loves* (Harcourt Brace, 1960), 8.

11. For more on this, see Tim Perry, "Forbid Them Not: The Place of Children in the Theology of Marriage," in *Human Sexuality and the Nuptial Mystery*, ed. Roy R. Jeal (Cascade, 2010), 148–64.

12. Rod Dreher, *The Benedict Option: A Strategy for Christians in a Post-Christian Nation* (Sentinel, 2017); *Live Not by Lies: A Manual for Christian Dissidents* (Sentinel, 2020).

Chapter 3: Gnosticism

1. Irenaeus, *Against Heresies* 1.23. The Ante-Nicene Fathers, volume 1, ed. Philip Schaff (Hendrickson, 1994), 347–48 (hereafter ANF).

2. The word translated "dwelt," ἐσκήνωσεν, in John 1:14 deliberately alludes to the tent of meeting, or tabernacle, in Exodus.

3. Irenaeus, *Against Heresies* 3.11.1; ANF 1:426.

4. Irenaeus, *Against Heresies* 3.3.4; ANF 1:416.

5. Irenaeus, *Against Heresies* 1.22; ANF 1:347.

6. Jaroslav Pelikan, *The Emergence of the Catholic Tradition (100–600)*, vol. 1 in *The Christian Tradition: A History of the Development of Christian Doctrine* (University of Chicago Press, 1975), 82.

7. The exception is Valentinian Christianity, whose major documents were discovered in Nag Hammadi in 1945. See *Valentinian Christianity: Texts and Translations*, trans. Geoffrey S. Smith (University of California Press, 2020), for a good translation of primary sources.

8. Pelikan, *Emergence of the Catholic Tradition*, 84.

9. For a full accounting of gnosticism, see Pheme Perkins, *Gnosticism and the New Testament* (Philadelphia: Fortress, 1993) and Roelof van den Broek, *Gnostic Religion in Antiquity* (Cambridge University Press, 2013).

10. Pelikan, *Emergence of the Catholic Tradition*, 85.

11. Pelikan, *Emergence of the Catholic Tradition*, 90.

12. For all the prattling among the chattering classes about anticolonialism, it amazes me how hard we find it to grasp that while large parts of Africa, Asia, and Eastern Europe might envy our prosperity, they regard our presuppositional materialism with scorn.

13. On the neognostic instrumentalization of the body, see Robert P. George, "Gnostic Liberalism," https://robertpgeorge.com/articles/gnostic-liberalism. On the phenomenon of transableism, see Ashley P. Taylor, "The Complicated Issue of Transableism," in *JSTOR Daily*, August 17, 2019, https://daily.jstor.org/the-complicated-issue-of-transableism.

14. See, for example, Justin Martyr, *The First Apology of Justin*.

15. Niebuhr, *Christ and Culture*, 87.

16. Though the story is ancient, found in Hindu, Jain, and Buddhist texts, it is retold in English by the Victorian poet John Godfrey Saxe as "The Blind Man and the Elephant." See John Godfrey Saxe, *The Poems of John Godfrey Saxe Complete in One Volume* (Ticknor and Fields, 1868), 259–61. In Saxe's version, the perspective of the king is taken up by the poet himself. Both seem unaware of that position's presumption, if not outright arrogance.

17. For their part, leaders in the early church could return fire as easily. Where the gnostics were secretive, they were public. Where the gnostic teachers were anonymous, their teachers could trace their lineage to the apostles. Where gnostic truths were hidden, the gospel was public truth: Jesus Christ born of the Virgin Mary, crucified under Pontius Pilate, and risen from the dead.

18. David Bebbington, *Evangelicalism in Modern Britain: A History from the 1730s to the 1980s* (London: Routledge, 1988); see also *The Evangelical Quadrilateral*, 2 vols. (Baylor University Press, 2021).

19. This found fullest expression in the journal *First Things* and the project known as Evangelicals and Catholics Together. See Timothy George and Thomas F. Guarino, eds., *Evangelicals and Catholics Together at Twenty: Vital Statements on Contested Topics* (Brazos, 2015).

20. Christian Smith and Melinda Lundquist Denton, *Soul Searching: The Religious and Spiritual Lives of American Teenagers* (Oxford University Press, 2005). See also the sequel, Christian Smith with Patricia Snel, *Souls in Transition: The Religious and Spiritual Lives of Emerging Adults* (Oxford University Press, 2009).

21. See James Emery White, *The Rise of the Nones: Understanding and Reaching the Religiously Unaffiliated* (Baker, 2014).

22. Stephen Bullivant, *Non-verts: The Making of Ex-Christian America* (Oxford University Press, 2022).

23. Arthur E. Farnsley II, "From the Rise of the 'Nones' to the Indifference of the 'Never Weres,'" in *Christianity Today*, November 2022, https://www.christianitytoday.com /ct/2022/december/nonverts-stephen-bullivant-nones-ex-christian.html.

24. F. D. E. Schleiermacher, *On Religion: Speeches to Its Cultured Despisers*. In *Cambridge Texts in the History of Philosophy*, ed. Richard Crouter (Cambridge University Press, 1996).

25. See Moore's Erasmus lecture, "Can the Religious Right Be Saved?" *First Things*, October 27, 2016, https://www. firstthings.com/media/can-the-religious-right-be-saved.

26. David P. Gushee, "On LGBT Equality, Middle Ground Is Disappearing," *Religion News Service*, August 22, 2016, https://religionnews.com/2016/08/22/on-lgbt-equality-middle-ground-is-disappearing.

27. At present, movies like *The Matrix* remain science fiction, but the "simulation hypothesis," that is, the idea that human beings are "simulations in some colossal video game," does appear to be gaining ground in some quarters. See Jay Pasachoff, "Are we living in a simulated universe?," January 31, 2017, https://www.nbcnews.com/mach/ features/are-we-living-simulated-universe-n713031. This is

a far more radical notion than the transhumanism heaven, in which human beings leave this world behind as much as possible, even uploading their consciousnesses into computers to attain "eternal life." On this, see Julien Musolino, Geordie Rose, and Michael Murray, "What Does It Mean to be Human? Ghosts and Machines," https://www.youtube.com/watch?time_continue=26&v=2IYR22ouDP8&embeds_euri=https%3A%2F%2Fwww.wycliffecollege.ca%2F&source_ve_path=MTM5MTE3LDE2NDk5LDIzODUx&feature=emb_title. The presentation by quantum computing entrepreneur and founder of D-Wave, Geordie Rose, is especially fascinating, even disturbing.

28. See Yascha Mounk, *The Identity Trap: Stories of Ideas and Power in Our Time* (Penguin, 2023).

29. For more on this, see Alvin Plantinga, *Where the Conflict Really Lies: Science, Religion, and Naturalism* (Oxford University Press, 2011).

30. C. S. Lewis, *The Abolition of Man* (Word on Fire Academic, 2021), 18. See also the superb commentary by Michael Ward, *After Humanity: A Guide to C. S. Lewis's* The Abolition of Man (Word on Fire Academic, 2021).

31. "The Order for Morning Prayer," The Book of Common Prayer 1662 (various editions).

32. Hendrik Kraemer, *The Christian Message in a Non-Christian World* (Edinburgh House, 1938).

33. It is the same point reiterated again and again in the writings of Lesslie Newbigin. See especially *The Gospel in a Pluralist Society* (Eerdmans, 1989), and *Proper Confidence* (Eerdmans, 1995).

34. C. S. Lewis, *The Silver Chair* (Geoffrey Bles, 1953).

35. Fourth, that is, in the order of publication. In the chronological ordering of the series, *The Silver Chair* is book six.

36. C. S. Lewis, *Silver Chair*, 159.

Chapter 4: Arianism

1.   G. K. Chesterton, *Orthodoxy* ch. 2, in *Heretics and Orthodoxy*, Lexham Classics (Lexham Press, 2017), 178.

2.   Thomas Aquinas, *Commentary on the Metaphysics* 12.9.19 (2566), https://isidore.co/aquinas/english/Metaphysics12 .htm#12.

3.   Rowan Williams, *Arius: Heresy and Tradition* (Darton, Longman and Todd, 1986), 1.

4.   John Behr, *The Nicene Faith*, part 1, vol. 2 of *Formation of Christian Theology* (St. Vladimir's Seminary Press, 2004), 131.

5.   These readings, with well-credentialed scholarly champions, are summarized in Behr, *Nicene Faith*, 132–33.

6.   The following paragraphs are especially indebted to Williams, *Arius*; Behr, *The Nicene Faith,* part 1; and Khaled Anatolios, *Retrieving Nicaea: The Development and Meaning of Trinitarian Doctrine* (Baker, 2011).

7.   Though the fluidity of what we call the Old Testament at this time must immediately be acknowledged, it certainly didn't seem to bother Origen, whose *Hexapla* set out six "versions" of the Hebrew Bible in parallel columns: the Hebrew text, a Greek transliteration thereof (with vowels added), and four Greek translations: Aquila, Symmachus, a revised version of the Septuagint, and Theodotion.

8.   Anatolios, *Retrieving Nicaea*, 16–17.

9.   Behr, *Nicene Faith*, 62.

10.   Jaroslav Pelikan, *The Emergence of the Catholic Tradition (100–600)*, vol. 1 in *The Christian Tradition: A History of the Development of Christian Doctrine* (University of Chicago Press, 1975), 198.

11.   Arius, *The Thalia* 1–2, quoted in Behr, *Nicene Faith*, 140.

12. H. G. Opitz, ed., *Athanasius Werke*, vol. 3, part 1, *Urkun-den zur Geschichte des Arianischen Streites* (De Gruyter, 1934), quoted in Behr, *Nicene Faith*, 135.

13. Arius, *Thalia* 5–7, quoted in Behr, *Nicene Faith*, 140.

14. Arius, *Thalia* 11–12, 32–34, quoted in Behr, *Nicene Faith*, 140–41.

15. Don't be distracted by recent debates about divine simplicity and impassibility; notice only that Arius and Eusebius, Athanasius and Alexander all affirmed them as constituent of the Christian doctrine of God.

16. Note Behr's criticism of Maurice Wiles, "In Defense of Arianism," in *Journal of Theological Studies* 13 (1962), 339–47, and R. C. Gregg and D. E. Groh, *Early Arianism: A View of Salvation* (Fortress, 1981) in *Nicene Faith*, 133–34.

17. There is a further wrinkle here that we will not explore: Arius appears to have taught that in the incarnation, the Logos *replaced* the human soul that animated the body of Jesus of Nazareth. Thus for Arius Jesus did not suffer according to this humanity in the unity of his person, as later theologians would aver, but in both (human) body and (semidivine) soul.

18. Pelikan, *Emergence of the Catholic Tradition*, 199.

19. Pelikan, *Emergence of the Catholic Tradition*, 199.

20. Matthew Avery Sutton, *Aimee Semple McPherson and the Resurrection of of Christian America* (Harvard University Press, 2007). See especially, "Marketing the Old-Time Religion" pp. 66–89, the reference to Hollywood appears on p. 70.

21. Kevin Kee, *Revivalists: Marketing the Gospel in English Canada, 1884–1957* (MQUP, 2006). The first chapter is titled "A Night at the Theatre."

22. It is certainly true that evangelical theologians are more conversant with trends and concerns and theologians outside the movement now than ever before. It is also true, however, that those evangelical theologians whose influence extends to theological conversation outside the movement can be counted on one hand: Kevin Vanhoozer, Alister McGrath, John Webster, Oliver O'Donovan, and Stanley Hauerwas (though Hauerwas may well bristle at the label).

23. Philip Melanchthon, *Loci Communes*, in *Melancthon and Bucer* (Library of Christian Classics), ed. Wilhelm Pauk (Westminster John Knox, 1969), 29.

24. John R. W. Stott, *The Cross of Christ* (InterVarsity Press, 1986). Some might object that I am unfairly ignoring the work of T. F. Torrance. I am not. Certainly Torrance was a sympathetic fellow traveler with evangelicals, especially toward the end of his life. But is it fair to group him with Packer, Stott, and Lloyd Jones as a British evangelical? Would he accept the designation without qualification? The answer to both questions, it seems to me, is no.

25. Rightly understood, penal substitutionary atonement means that the Father sends the Son in the power of the Spirit to bear the divine wrath against sin and so take it away. It is, in other words, a triune act. For the sake of love, *God* bears his own wrath that sin might be destroyed and humanity redeemed. Penal substitution does not present the anger of the Father unjustly directed at the innocent, nobly willing Son, with the Spirit strangely absent. When critics take aim at the doctrine articulated this way, they are not aiming at penal substitution itself but an abhorrent caricature thereof.

26. Friedrich Schleiermacher, *The Christian Faith: A New Translation and Critical Edition*, trans. Terrence N. Tice and Catherine L. Kelsey (Philadelphia: Westminster John Knox, 2016).

27. A helpful introduction to the notion of *Gefühl* (which remains slippery in Schleiermacher) can be found in Julia Lamm, "The Early Philosophical Roots of Schleiermacher's Notion of Gefühl, 1788–1794," in *Harvard Theological Review* 87 (2011): 67–105.

28. The phrase is Thomas G. Long's, in "The Binary Christianity of Marcus Borg," *The Christian Century*, July 7, 2017, https://www.christiancentury.org/review/binary-christianity-of-marcus-borg.

29. George Tyrrell, *Christianity at the Cross-Roads* (London: Longmans, Green and Co., 1910), 44.

30. If that. The second verse of the hymn is often omitted in hymnals or slides, since it's both doctrinally and metrically complex.

31. It follows that our "fighting for Jesus" should be the first sign to us that we've lost him.

32. This is the core of Rowan Williams's disagreement with him. Compare John Henry Newman, *The Arians of the Fourth Century* (London: Longmans, Green and Co., 1833); Rowan Williams, *Arius*, 2nd ed. (London: SCM, 2002).

Chapter 5: Pelagianism

1. Jaroslav Pelikan, *The Emergence of the Catholic Tradition (100–600)*, vol. 1 in *The Christian Tradition: A History of the Development of Christian Doctrine* (University of Chicago Press, 1975), 281.

2. See Friedrich Nietzsche, *The Birth of Tragedy*, trans. Douglas Smith (Oxford University Press, 2008).

3. Origen, *On Prayer* 10.2, in Tertullian, Cyprian, and Origen, *On the Lord's Prayer*, ed. John Behr, trans. Alistair Stewart-Sykes, Popular Patristics Series 29 (St Vladimir's Seminary Press, 2004), 133.

4. Augustine, *The City of God* 5.9, The Nicene and Post-Nicene Fathers, series 1, volume 2, ed. Philip Schaff (Hendrickson, 1994), 91 (hereafter NPNF).

5. Pelikan, *Emergence of the Catholic Tradition*, 282.

6. Pelikan, *Emergence of the Catholic Tradition*, 284.

7. Stephen A. Cooper, *Augustine for Armchair Theologians* (Louisville, KY: Westminster John Knox, 2002), 208.

8. See Jordan Peterson, *Twelve Rules for Life: An Antidote to Chaos* (Toronto: Penguin Random House Canada, 2018); *Beyond Order: Twelve More Rules for Life* (Toronto: Penguin Random House Canada, 2021).

9. See Jennifer Ebbeler, *Disciplining Christians: Correction and Community in Augustine's Letters*, Oxford Studies in Late Antiquity (Oxford University Press, 2012), especially chapter 5, "The Retrospective Correction of Pelagius," 191–225.

10. Pelikan, *Emergence of the Catholic Tradition*, 313.

11. Augustine, *The Confessions of St. Augustine*, trans. E. B. Pusey, Everyman's Library (Dent & Sons, 1907), 8.9; pp. 165–66.

12. Augustine, The Confessions of St. Augustine, trans. E. B. Pusey, 8.11, p. 168.

13. Augustine, *The Confessions of St. Augustine*, trans. E. B. Pusey, 8.12, p. 170.

14. Augustine, *The Confessions of St. Augustine*, trans. E. B. Pusey, 8.12, p. 171.

15. Pelikan, *Emergence of the Catholic Tradition*, 315.

16. Augustine, O*n the Proceedings of Pelagius* 11 (NPNF 1, vol. 5, 193).

17. Augustine, *On Original Sin* 19 (NPNF 1, vol. 5, 244).

18. *The New English Hymnal* (Canterbury Press, 1986), no. 488.

19. This old legend is, perhaps surprisingly, within the realm of possibility, given the known trading routes of the first-century Roman world. But there is no direct evidence.

20. See Peter Porter, *The English Poets: From Chaucer to Edward Thomas* (Penguin Random House, 1974), 198.

21. Christopher Rowland, "William Blake: A Visionary for Our Time," in *Open Democracy*, November 27, 2007, https://www.opendemocracy.net/en/william_blake_a_visionary_for_our_time.

22. Leo XIII, *Rerum Novarum* (May 15, 1891). https://www.vatican.va/content/leo-xiii/en/encyclicals/documents/hf_l-xiii_enc_15051891_rerum-novarum.html.

23. Anselm of Canterbury, *Cur Deus Homo* 1.21, in *Proslogium; Monologium; An Appendix in Behalf of the Fool by Gaunilon; and Cur Deus Homo*, trans. Sidney Norton Deane (Open Court Publishing, 1926), 228–30.

24. See Leslie Newbigin, *Foolishness to the Greeks: The Gospel and Western Culture* (Eerdmans, 1988). Newbigin, whom it was my great privilege to meet not long before he died, was a prophet for our time, and his works, *The Gospel in a Pluralist Society, The Open Secret, Proper Confidence*, along with *Foolishness to the Greeks*, are an authentic political manifesto for our time.

Chapter 6: Donatism

1. We could also give examples of orthodox champions who were, in fact, skunks. In this group, the figure of Cyril of Alexandria, champion of the Theotokos, looms especially large. "After his death, one exuberant writer, proclaiming that the living were finally happy to be rid of him, sug-

gested that the undertakers place an extra stone on Cyril's grave, in case the disheartened dead should try to send him back." See Michael G. Azar, *Exegeting the Jews: The Early Reception of the Johannine Jews* (Brill, 2016), 154.

2. Justo L. González, *The Story of Christianity*, vol. 1, *The Early Church to the Dawn of the Reformation*, rev. ed. (Harper Collins, 2010), 173–74.

3. González, *Early Church to the Dawn of the Reformation*, 174.

4. Jaroslav Pelikan, *The Finality of Jesus Christ in an Age of Universal History: A Dilemma of the Third Century* (John Knox Press, 1966), 32.

5. Augustine, *In Answer to the Letters of Petilian the Donatist* 1.4 (NPNF 1, vol. 4, 520–21).

6. Augustine, *In Answer to the Letters of Petilian the Donatist* 3.43 (NPNF 1, vol. 4, 614).

7. Augustine, *On Baptism Against the Donatists* 6.15 (NPNF 1, vol. 4, 484).

8. The standard work on fundamentalism remains George Marsden's *Fundamentalism and American Culture*, now forty years old. See George Marsden, *Fundamentalism and American Culture*, third edition (Oxford University Press, 2022).

9. See John Fea's old but still very helpful article, "Understanding the Changing Facade of Twentieth-Century American Protestant Fundamentalism: Toward a Historical Definition," *Trinity Journal* (Fall 1994): 181–99.

10. John Paul II, *Fides et Ratio* (September 14, 1998). https://www.vatican.va/content/john-paul-ii/en/encyclicals/documents/hf_jp-ii_enc_14091998_fides-et-ratio.html.

11. Oliver O'Donovan, *On The Thirty Nine Articles: A Conversation with Tudor Christianity* (Latimer House, 1986).

12. See Augustine, *Letter 93 to Vincentius* (NPNF 1, vol. 1, 382–401).